GARBAGE PIZZA, PATCHWORK QUILTS, AND MATH MAGIC

*Stories about Teachers
Who Love to Teach and
Children Who Love to Learn*

SUSAN OHANIAN

W. H. Freeman and Company
New York

The views expressed in publications funded by the Exxon Education Foundation are those of the author and do not necessarily reflect the views of the staff, officers, or trustees of the Foundation.

Except for pp. 44, 45, and 49, the artwork was drawn by children who participated in the Exxon Education Foundation K–3 Mathematics Specialist Program in association with the National Council of Teachers of Mathematics (NCTM). Special thanks to these children.

Library of Congress Cataloging-in-Publication Data

Ohanian, Susan.
    Garbage pizza, patchwork quilts, and math magic: Stories about teachers who love to teach and children who love to learn / Susan Ohanian.
      p. cm.
    Includes bibliographical references and index.
    ISBN 0-7167-2360-3
    1. Mathematics—Study and teaching (Primary)   I. Title.
QA135.5.O33   1993
372.7—dc20   92-26094
                                               CIP

Printed in the United States of America

1 2 3 4 5 6 7 8 9 0   VB   9 9 8 7 6 5 4 3 2

Contents

Preface

Call me teacher. Twenty-plus years of hanging around classrooms defines who I am and what I bring to this book. I am the sort of person who shuts herself up in a room full of eight-year-olds 182 days a year—and not only lives to tell about it but rejoices in the telling. This book has a point of view: it is opinionated and, I hope, passionate. I left the classroom after twenty years because I wanted the teacher's voice to be heard. I was fed up by the commentary that surrounds education. Literally 98.43 percent of the people who write and talk publicly about education are strangers in a strange land.

In the past I have written about what I know best: my own classroom. The challenge in this book was to write about other people's classrooms. After poking around in classrooms across the country for one year, I devoted a second year to figuring out how to describe what I had seen. My goal has been to give the committed, caring, sometimes quirky teacher a chance to be seen and heard. I hope that when parents and politicians, and anybody else who cares about education, get an insider's view of what goes on in a few classrooms, they will be hungry for more. I hope that after taking my schoolhouse tour the reader might just be inspired to seek out a few teachers and talk to them. Talk to them and listen, too.

The Exxon Education Foundation financed my travels—and never once offered any suggestion about what I should write. They did not even get so much as an inkling of what the book would look like until the publisher sent them a copy. I mention this because it cuts deeply to one of the messages of this book: as a longtime teacher I am awestruck when a giant corporation or anybody else trusts a teacher to do the job she or he was hired to do. Such trust is foreign to most education overseers—from the Secretary of Education to Congress to state governors to local boards of education. Of course, teachers themselves are the first to express astonishment that a large and esteemed foundation hired a teacher to write about education. What a notion! Asking a teacher to examine and report on education is definitely an idea few government, media, or other institutions have tried.

Poet-farmer-professor Wendell Berry says that trees on a farm are a sign of the farmer's "long-term good intentions toward the place." This is a good metaphor for the K–3 Math Specialist Project described in this book. The Exxon Education Foundation takes this long-term view. The administrators of the Foundation are not looking to raise standardized test scores in mathematics next year or even five years hence. They believe that by providing pattern blocks (and other hands-on materials) for kindergartners and time for training and collegial talk for teachers, they are helping to develop the mathematically savvy citizens our country needs in the twenty-first century. The Foundation's commitment to this long-term view is buttressed by the professional leadership provided by the National Council of Teachers of Mathematics, whose two documents, *Curriculum and Evaluation Standards for School Mathematics* and *Professional Standards for Teaching Mathematics,* set goals for reforming elementary and secondary mathematics instruction.

I have one regret about this book: that many good classrooms I have visited are not mentioned. It is rare to walk into a classroom and see that "telling incident" unfold before one's eyes. I am astounded that I saw as many of those incidents as I did, and I know that for every one I describe, I missed ten thousand equally wonderful moments by a minute, a day, a month. Veteran teachers know that teaching, like farming, requires a lot of faith. A teacher must learn how to wait quietly. So must an education observer/commentator—which explains why, I guess, the media cover education so badly. Most of the time nothing seems to be happening in classrooms, and we don't have any educational time-lapse photography to reveal the miracle of children blooming. Knowing that I had missed most such telling moments, I asked teachers to send me their classroom stories. When very few responded, I was disappointed and even angry: How was I going to write a book if teachers didn't tell me their stories? Then I realized I had asked the impossible. A teacher can't teach and reflect at the same time; she can't step out of her teacherliness to "observe herself" and then philosophize about how her day went. She certainly has no time to send off reports. Perhaps even more to the point is that teachers aren't politicians; self-praise is foreign to their nature. Teachers do not shout "Look at me! I have a wonderful classroom, and I'm going to change the world!" Instead, we teachers shut our doors and do our best; our highest dream is to be left alone to do our jobs. But just as children who are not cherished don't know how to cherish themselves, the same must be said of teachers. My real regret is that some good teachers won't find their stories in this book and therefore won't feel cherished. I hope for two things: I hope these unsung teachers will rejoice in the stories of our colleagues and I hope they will feel inspired to tell their own stories one day.

Acknowledgments

First of all, I'd like to express my amazement that an organization like the Exxon Education Foundation would choose someone like me to write a book about math. For that, I thank Mike Dooley, the Foundation's program officer for the K–3 project, and Marilyn Burns, a teacher's teacher. Mike took a giant risk and gave me as much room to find my topic as the Foundation gives its math specialists for their "method." He continued to profess faith and optimism every time my self-doubts surfaced. Marilyn has a unique ability to share ideas and to help people of all ages grow. I am grateful for her rigor, her professionalism, her faith in children and their teachers, and her belief that the world is big enough for many stars to shine. I am grateful also to Pat Hess who, as the connecting link between the Exxon Education Foundation and classrooms across the country, holds everything together. We visited many classrooms together, rejoicing in what we saw and sharing dreams of things getting even better. I'm grateful to the teachers and children who welcomed me into their classrooms, who so proudly explained their work. Finally, I am even grateful to Hans for that calculus book he gave me the first year we were married. His refusal to believe that someone with a master's degree in medieval literature couldn't do math taught me a lot more than differential equations. But surprisingly enough, I learned them too.

Introduction

Once people realize I'm not joking, that I really have spent the past year sitting in primary math classrooms in more than twenty states, they always offer their sympathy. Watching children struggle with mathematics is definitely not most people's idea of a good time. Since I started working on this book I have discovered that everyone has that same nightmare: arriving late for a final exam you haven't studied for. Usually it's a math exam. I've discovered the real terror is not failing the exam; the real terror is having to take the math class again. The pain of those good old math basics of endless column addition, subtraction from zero, and algebraic formulas that could have been Sanskrit for all the sense we made of them seems to stick with us forever. I understand people's apprehension about math, even math at the second grade level. But I bring good news: mathematics is changing; it is changing a lot.

Most of us acknowledge that learning mathematics is important, but we also hope that someone else will do the learning. Participants in a 1990 Gallup poll responded that mathematics education in high school is more crucial than any other subject, nosing out even English by four percentage points. A concerned public says that math is crucial, and yet more than half of today's crop of high school graduates have not taken any math courses past tenth grade. Disturbing? Yes. A new trend? No. High school graduates of decades past, the very people who told Gallup pollsters that mathematics is the most important high school course, didn't even get as far as tenth grade math.

So what's happening? If we believe in the importance of mathematics, why don't we practice what we preach? Why do we stop taking math courses as soon as we can? For one thing, children tend to inherit academic attitudes, both positive and negative, from their parents, and a whole lot of parents have negative attitudes about mathematics. Eddie's mom was fairly typical. Though very concerned about Eddie's progress in reading, she nonetheless dismissed his struggles in mathematics with an airy, "Oh, I never could do math either." I begged Eddie's mom not to regale her son with stories of her own math failure. Eddie had not yet learned addition or subtraction facts, and every time I tried to show him double digit subtraction, he would whine, "I don't know how to do that." It was clear that Eddie's mom did not expect him to master any of this arcane information, and children have a way of living up to our expectations.

We teachers know that we also pass on academic attitudes to our students, subtle—even subliminal—attitudes not found in textbooks. How could it be otherwise, when most elementary teachers don't feel any better about mathematics than the public at large? One of the very scary facts about being a teacher is that every second of every day we teach who we are, and if nothing extraordinary intercedes to transform us, we teach the way we were taught.

But for many teachers something is interceding. My year-long journey into math classrooms across the country has given me an inside look at some profound shifts in mathematics instruction. I found thousands of kindergartners and first, second, and third graders discovering number patterns, exploring geometry, and learning to collect, organize, and interpret data. I saw kindergartners create graphs of the types of sandwiches they brought for lunch, watched third graders make tessellations, and heard young children talk about Fibonacci patterns, probability, and game theory. These children's teachers realize that the arithmetic that was good enough for Grandpa is definitely not good enough for Johnny—or Eddie. I felt challenged and exhilarated by what I observed.

My teacher friends are anxious to find out about new methods, and they ask me to share with them the good ideas I discover in my travels. But if I have learned anything in my twenty-five years as a teacher, it is that good ideas are never enough. I've lost track of the number of teaching techniques someone brought into my school district, promising to reform educational practices—and raise student test scores. Smart technology, for example, has been lurking in dark corridors since that day in 1965 when I first sat behind a teacher's desk: efficient teaching machines, closed-circuit television, interactive videos, computer networking. This technology has been no more effective in bringing lasting school reform than the new textbooks, the seven-step plans for teaching a lesson, and the countless strategies guaranteeing to raise student self-esteem, end drug abuse, and prevent pregnancy—as well as raise those test scores.

In the end, solutions to the problems of education turn out to be more complex than what a technology or a panacea can supply. I know that teaching is a humanistic endeavor, relying on human interaction and human choices. I used to say, "Not in reading, but maybe those machines will work for math class." But my year-long journey has convinced me that mathematics education, when done right, is no less a humanistic endeavor than reading or social studies. You can take an innovative technique for increasing student understanding of multiplication, reproduce it on a computer program, and give it to every third grader in the nation. And what will you have? Without a smart and sensitive teacher reacting and prodding and shifting and altering and inspiring, you'll have just another sound-and-light-show workbook. Successful schools don't import lots of quick-fix trivia for second grade math bulletin boards or third grade homework worksheets; rather, successful schools take a long view, offering courses that develop their teachers' own mathematical understanding.

I began my study for the Exxon Education Foundation thinking that my job would be to record what I saw; I did not expect to be changed by it. I saw myself as merely an observer, never imagining that I would become a learner along the way. I was wrong. I have learned a lot. I've discovered how the words other people choose affect the job you do; I've seen how a term such as *primary math specialist* can transform a teacher, her school, and the community. A community has different expectations of a math specialist than it does of a third grade teacher. A math specialist develops different expectations of herself.

For more than twenty years I tried to convince myself that a good teacher could do it alone; she could educate herself and keep her own flame burning brightly, nourished only by her students and her own intellectualism. But I realize now that teaching need not be an isolating profession. My visits to Albuquerque and Tucson and Orlando and East Baton Rouge and Milwaukee and Bellevue have shown me that successful school districts provide a structure that helps teachers learn from and support one another as they discover together how to become better mathematics teachers. I have seen firsthand that when second grade teachers are enrolled in geometry and calculus courses, they walk a little taller. When teachers learn more about mathematics, this knowledge spreads from their own curriculum into other teachers' classrooms, administrators' offices, and parents' meetings.

Some cynics predict that the current mathematics reform movement is doomed to fail just as past attempts at reform failed. It is hard to remain optimistic when you've seen as many reforms die as I have. Nonetheless, I remain optimistic about this one. I see a difference in this "new" reform: teachers are finally coming in to their own professionally.

Lessons for the Ivory Tower

I was amazed to discover something else this past year: some universities are capable of change. They are insisting that even professors can become learners. Very different from the 1970s, when I spent four years being "retrained" by professors at a prestigious teacher-education institution. These pedagogues never once entered my classroom or talked with one of my students. After a couple of years, they finally wanted to see me teach—but I had to transfer from my class of lousy readers in elementary school to a class of gifted students in high school. I taught a dog-and-pony show for the benefit of the professors and then went back to my own classroom. When I tried to show a professor the work of my real students, he shook his head sadly and asked me when I was going to stop "wasting my time" teaching elementary school and join them at the university. I guess I was supposed to feel honored by the invitation, but I felt only outrage that he and his colleagues had such contempt for my life's work. That ended my retraining—I quit. I knew then, as I know now, that the work of an elementary school teacher is emotionally difficult and intellectually challenging, that it is work that should be honored, not belittled.

The reform efforts of the 1960s and early 1970s failed because of professorial hubris; academic reformers approached teachers with the attitude of messengers bringing revelation. It never occurred to those academics that teachers could be colleagues, capable of contributing to the theory and practice of good instruction. We were seen as so much expendable baggage needed by the university to gets its federal grant money. If one of their ready-to-wear lessons didn't work, then something was wrong with us teachers and with the children. The professors made no effort to understand our daily working lives; they made no effort to understand how difficult it is for teachers to change their own attitudes, beliefs, and skills, let alone to sustain those changes without any kind of institutional support.

Supporting Change by Supporting Teacher Change Agents

The Exxon Education Foundation decided to get involved in elementary mathematics education after examining the mathematics performance of this country's young adults. A 1986 national assessment showed only about half of all seventeen-year-olds in the United States were proficient in math of a junior high school level; only half of the eight hundred doctorates in mathematics awarded each year by universities in the United States go to United States citizens. Then, after studying research revealing that people's lifelong attitudes toward learning are formed in the primary grade and that children "turn off" mathematics by fourth grade, the Foundation decided to concentrate on math education in kindergarten through the third grade, hoping that if very young children are "hooked" on mathematics, they will stay hooked forever. The Foundation sent out a call for proposals for something they called a *K–3 math specialist*, inviting school districts, universities, and individual teachers to submit their ideas on how these math specialists could reform mathematics education in primary schools.

As a veteran of trying to decipher guidelines sent out by the U.S. Department of Education, I view this call for proposals as a stroke of genius. The guidelines were very short on policies and procedures, very long on possibilities. The Foundation used the term *K–3 math specialist* without specifying what it meant. Then they funded each proposal with a planning grant, providing money for teachers, administrators, parents, and university personnel to sit down for a year and decide just what a primary grade mathematics specialist's job might be and what this specialist might do. After a year, each school whose planning grant showed any sort of promise was given an additional implementation grant, money to get both the math specialists and the new ideas into primary classrooms.

What is unique and, to my mind, extraordinarily prescient about the Exxon Education Foundation's determination to introduce and sustain innovation in primary grade mathematics education is that it has put all its eggs into one basket. And the professional organization of mathematics teachers, the National Council of Teachers of Mathematics (the NCTM), is holding that basket. Quite patient about giving local districts time and space to find their own needs, the Foundation gets assertive about one thing: the Foundation wants participating teachers to become involved with the NCTM. When Pat Hess, the liaison between the Exxon Education Foundation, the NCTM, and the schools, visits a project school, she asks, "How many teachers went to the NCTM annual convention? How many are going to the next one?" If a district isn't sending teachers to the national convention, Hess pushes for the teachers to at least attend the regional convention.

Because most elementary teachers teach all subjects, they tend not to join any professional organization with special affiliation to reading or social studies or mathematics or whatever. Teachers may read library copies of professional journals, but the NCTM is the first professional organization most teachers in the K–3 Math Project have ever joined. The importance of this professional affiliation cannot be overemphasized. Any doubters should talk to a fifteen-year-veteran teacher after she returns to the classroom after her first professional convention, feeling renewed and, for the first time, professional.

Another remarkably smart move by the Exxon Education Foundation is to praise change wherever and however it occurs. This ranges from funding system-wide mathematics reform in Orlando, Florida, to buying materials so parents could make geometric pattern blocks for one school in Kentucky. The Foundation sends out a *K–3 Math Specialist Newsletter* to all schools, in which Pat Hess highlights student work from the classrooms she visits and recommends professional articles, films, and materials to teachers. This newsletter celebrates the small seeds of change when they occur, celebrating, for instance, the use of pattern blocks rather than asking why the teachers aren't using Cuisenaire rods and geoboards too. I have seen Hess nearly bite through her tongue to keep from telling a teacher, "These children should be using a calculator to solve a column addition problem." Later, she explains her restraint. "That teacher is doing fine. She has the calculators in the room. That is the crucial beginning. She'll learn to use them; she doesn't need to be told. We have to be patient." The newsletter that Hess edits will let this teacher know that she is a part of a national community of K–3 mathematics specialists. And Hess will discuss ways to use calculators in first grade classes in the next issue.

This is not to say that the Foundation is looking for uniformity. Even though all K–3 math specialists share certain assumptions and materials, differences abound, and anyone who wants to come to grips with what's happening in American schooling needs to appreciate that there are nearly as many differences among meritorious teachers and their schools as there are similarities. Accordingly, the Foundation is equally enthusiastic about the unique qualities of projects in Bellevue and East Baton Rouge; nobody suggests they should copy each other. The fact that neither bears a whole lot of resemblance to successful projects in Milwaukee or Albuquerque is just fine.

People at the Exxon Education Foundation express amazement that teachers should care what they think. "These teachers are the experts," insists Mike Dooley, the Foundation's program officer for the K–3 Math Project. But I keep telling him that teachers aren't used to being valued as experts; they're used to being told how lousy their schools are. Neither are teachers accustomed to being invited to Washington and Dallas to attend weekend seminars on new trends in mathematics. But when a company like Exxon keeps saying you are a professional, you start to believe it. You discover it's a good feeling.

NCTM's Curriculum and Evaluation Standards

Curriculum and Evaluation Standards for School Mathematics was published by the NCTM in 1989, receiving high acclaim from national leaders in education, business and industry, and government alike. Supporters of these *Standards* range from the U.S. Secretary of Education and the Institute of Electrical and Electronics Engineers to the American Association of Retired Persons, the American Association of University Women, and the American Bankers Association.

The *Standards* not only create a vision of what it means to be mathematically competent "in a world where mathematics is rapidly growing and is extensively being applied in diverse fields" but also outline a set of goals to "guide the revision of the school mathematics curriculum." For kindergarten through the fourth grade, the *Standards* recommend that teachers place less emphasis on complex pencil-and-paper calculations and more emphasis on number sense; less emphasis on solitary rote memorization of rules and more emphasis on learning to work together with concrete, manipulative materials; less emphasis on single-answer, one-method problems and more emphasis on the ability to explain mathematical thinking and writing. Pointing out that in the real world most problems we encounter are not neatly arranged for us the way they are in textbooks, the *Standards* underscore the importance of students finding mathematical problems in everyday situations and developing a variety of strategies to solve those problems. One of the most striking changes is that the *Standards* put the teacher of the 1990s in charge.

Any teacher who survived the prevailing education dogma of the mid-1970s through the 1980s knows that a lot of consultants made a lot of money selling school districts on the concept of teachers as managers, as systems experts. With its *Standards*, the NCTM places the teacher back in the center of the classroom. The *Standards* are teacher-dependent in the best sense of the word, stating categorically that the teacher must be a professional: an informed, specialized decision-maker. Central to the *Standards* is not a text or a program or a strategy; central to the *Standards* is the expert practitioner.

As I traveled around the country poking into primary grade mathematics classrooms, as I talked with teachers over the phone and looked at the student work they sent me, I became convinced that I am witnessing a revolution. I keep asking Pat Hess and Marilyn Burns, the teachers' teacher who is, no doubt, the single person most influential in transforming the way teachers across the country approach mathematics instruction, "What's going to happen when people find out what you're doing to arithmetic?" They laugh.

Back to the Basics or on to the Revolution?

In a political climate that put Professor E. D. Hirsch's "back to the basics" prescriptions on best-seller lists and on the cover of at least one news magazine, the media has paid scant attention to the size and passion of the "new mathematics" movement that not only runs counter to the traditional approach but also breaks all the political/religious/social rules about teachers' not taking risks, not rocking the boat. In *What Your First Grader Needs to Know* and *What Your Second Grader Needs to Know* (stay tuned for the third and the fourth grades), Hirsch has produced a series of math prescriptions that barely acknowledge the calculator and never mention the computer, number sense, or the importance of communicating mathematical ideas. Instead, Hirsch stresses the importance of practice and more practice, rote memorization, and speed. He even insists that second graders should learn roman numerals. Hirsch limits problem solving to defining for children the one correct method for getting the one possible answer to the comfortable kind of textbook problem that Grandpa would recognize. That is, Grandpa will feel comfortable because if Johnny's math looks familiar, then it must be okay. Never mind that most of our grandfathers did not progress to a higher mathematics that required understanding rather than rote responses. Hirsch insists that if students practice a skill long enough, they will become proficient at it. He assumes that understanding follows proficiency. The NCTM disagrees, publishing the *Standards* to explain why;

the Exxon Education Foundation disagrees, funding the K–3 math specialists to find a better way.

I look at Hirsch's simplistic, rearview-mirror approach to arithmetic and realize what a tough job teachers face. You can't buy the NCTM's vision of deep-rooted number sense in K mart, and even if the *Standards* were available in mass market distribution, how many people would spend $30 on a philosophical/pedagogical position paper strictly on math when Hirsch offers workbook problems for the whole curriculum—at half the price?

Although plenty of people will step forward to complain about a third grade teacher who doesn't force her students through the time-honored ritual of memorizing times tables, few eyebrows were raised when a professor of English literature, who offers no evidence he has ever taught elementary school mathematics, created a mathematics curriculum imperative. Although the superficiality of Hirsch's argument is frustrating to teachers, his curriculum is well suited to the back-to-basics sound bite. His core list garners strong support from a nostalgic public that is convinced that things used to be better. Indeed, Hirsch has a talent for making people over forty feel that good education stopped the minute they graduated from high school.

Hirsch and the National Council of Teachers of Mathematics do agree on one thing, however: mathematics education in this country needs a major overhaul. Hirsch looks with longing to the time when youngsters still learned their math facts. He is convinced the United States is now in trouble because teachers are neglecting those basic algorithms. Likewise, with its eye toward the future, looking to the challenge of the twenty-first century, the NCTM also believes that the United States is in trouble with mathematics. But the NCTM blames this trouble on the teachers who have filled their classrooms with the very skill-drills that Hirsch claims they abandoned decades ago. Hirsch wants computation in primary grades; the NCTM calls for computation, estimation, geometry, and spatial sense, measurement, statistics and probability, graphing, patterns, and relationships. Contradicting Hirsch, the NCTM insists that we need a basic number sense, something our students fail to achieve because too much classroom time is spent on rote memorization.

People Who Won't Be Fooled

You may be able to fool a lot of people a lot of the time, and a solid percentage of our citizens may wear permanent blinders. But no one is picketing the K–3 Math Project schools to bring back Grandpa's skill-drill workbooks, and I think I know why. Parent involvement is a big part of the project schools' mission, and parents who are informed and involved become enthusiastic partners in helping their children learn math for the twenty-first century. These parents are looking ahead and not back. An event known as Family Math Night, on which students bring their parents to school and "do" hands-on math with them, is a sell-out in projects all over the country—from Ford Heights, Illinois, to Columbia, Missouri, to Bellevue, Washington. Teachers from Irvine to Auburn report waiting lists of eager parent participants. Parents who experience the thrill of understanding the real mathematics underlying a rote procedure they memorized years ago are not eager to join a petition drive to substitute skill-drill worksheets for the manipulative materials that help their children understand, say, the geometric properties of multiplication. These parents remember their own math agony in school and don't want to see it perpetuated in their children.

Another benefit for the K–3 math specialists is the magic of the Exxon name. Every time a newsletter goes home or an invitation to Family Math Night is issued, the Exxon name is displayed prominently. Teachers feel more comfortable taking a risk in their curriculum when they can tell parents that this change is being sponsored both spiritually and financially by a giant corporation.

The Foundation stresses the importance of information, providing funds for K–3 Math Projects to communicate with one another and with the parents they serve. Each project issues a newsletter to parents, containing sample student work as well as explanations of the *Standards* and suggesting ways parents can help. I look at this newsletter as a sort of shareholders' quarterly report and wonder if this sort of thing isn't what the schools shouldn't be learning from industry. As parents see what their children can do, they are not so concerned about abolishing the old arithmetic of "Readin', 'Ritin', and 'Rithmetic," the arithmetic that makes people wince and say, "Oh, I never was any good in math." These parents welcome the mathematics revolution.

What Teaching Math Means Now

In one sense, the better teacher you are, the scarier teaching becomes. Experienced teachers realize that children's learning isn't confined to just that 40-minute segment in the plan book labeled "math period." Just as a teacher teaches every second of the day, with her every intonation and gesture, children never stop learning. They may not be learning the lesson the teacher thinks she's teaching, but they are nonetheless learning some thing all the time. And so teachers work to provide a rich environment of mathematical possibility, an environment that helps students approach a concept such as multiplication from a variety of directions. For example, some children more readily see the number relationships of repeated addition, while others more quickly understand the spatial relationships of a geometric model or the patterns generated by a calculator. Teachers are learning to accommodate and build on all these differing approaches rather than insisting on one "right" method.

Successful and highly commended teachers with twenty years of experience are rethinking their curriculum. They are quick to point out that they have foresworn the old arithmetic; now, they insist, they teach mathematics.

Where Are We Going?

When I started this project, I thought that I was going to document the details of the changing content of mathematics instruction, introducing lay readers to the mysteries and marvels of pattern blocks, Unifix cubes, and so on. And those stories are included in this book. But early in my journey, I began to realize that how Sarah and Eddie learn their multiplication facts in a given school is inextricably entwined with issues that on the surface don't seem to have a whole lot to do with number facts. I also found that watching the children in action was not enough— I needed to talk to principals and parents as well. I wanted to ask them how they grapple with the fact that a school can't separate its approach to mathematics rituals from its attitude toward child development, evaluation, teacher autonomy, and genuine parent participation.

I saw for myself that institutionalized change is neither accidental nor haphazard, that it occurs in districts where there is a framework for administrators, teachers, and parents to work and learn new things together—with the children and for the children. As parents see what their children can do, they become willing and even anxious to relinquish the old methods. Significantly, the most successful projects put an emphasis on the verbs: children "doing" mathematics. Whether it's first graders in Irvine writing their own math book or third graders in Tucson designing candy boxes, children are "living" math. A relatively small amount of money can produce extraordinary results. Whether it's parents in Kentucky making mathematics manipulatives, or parents in Illinois "guesstimating" the amount of punch they need to make for their meeting, or teachers in Tucson meeting once a month to talk and think and plan, across the country, children and teachers and parents are taking charge. I echo what Marilyn Burns said to a group of third grade teachers in Berkeley who had come from all over California to learn how to replace multiplication facts memorization with multiplication understanding: "It's an exciting time to be involved in mathematics education." Absolutely.

1

Learning Mathematics:
Keeping an Eye
on the Baby and
the Bathwater

Mary Bacon teaches kindergarten at the Goodwood Elementary School in East Baton Rouge, Louisiana. When she asks her students to draw pictures showing the number of people in their families, the results are telling. They provide a picture of the developmental range in Mary Bacon's class—and in any kindergarten classroom—a range that becomes wider as students move through school.

Although Daniel tells his teacher that there are two grown-ups and three children in his family, he draws five children. Daniel is the youngest child in the class—ten months younger than Julie, who is one of the oldest. Bacon reports that Julie is as "mature, creative, and self-motivated" in all her schoolwork as her family drawing might lead us to suppose. When we look at Daniel's drawing, however, that catchall faculty room word comes to mind: *immature*. Certainly it is clear that at this time Daniel is not performing at the same level as Julie. But teachers like Mary Bacon are beginning to ask themselves, why should he be? What is the value of comparing Daniel with Julie? Teachers are beginning to say that maybe it makes more sense to judge Daniel's work today with the work he did yesterday; they are beginning to say that maybe it is better to use the work Daniel does today to plan for what he will work on tomorrow. Teachers are saying maybe it is better to assess Daniel's growth over time rather than to insist he play catch-up with Julie.

Daniel, a kindergartner, draws his family.

Julie, a kindergartner, draws her family.

Parents are learning, too. When personnel at a school in northern California notified the mother of a four-and-a-half-year-old that her daughter had "failed" a pre-kindergarten screening, the mother questioned the verdict. School personnel administering the kindergarten entrance exam reported that the child sucked her thumb and was "immature." "Of course she's immature," agreed the mother when she took her protest to a school board meeting. "At four-and-a-half years of age what should she be if not immature?" This mother wanted to know who sets these absolute rules for four-and-a-half-year-olds' behavior. She pointed out that nobody tries to set such rules for forty-four-and-a-half-year-olds. This parent asked, "Who decides that four-year-olds who suck their thumbs aren't kindergarten material?" Across the country in Pennsylvania, another parent questioned similar policy that decreed her son should "wait a year" before starting kindergarten because he couldn't skip and was small for his age, small stature being acceptable for a female, decreed the gatekeepers, but not for a male.

Tending the Flock Rather Than Segregating the Buzzards

One of the often repeated tenets of education is "start where they are," meaning that teachers need to understand and appreciate what their students already know so they can develop appropriate educational programs. In the jargon of the faculty room, we need to know our students so we can "meet their needs." For some teachers, this means examining standardized test scores. In September, a second grade teacher, say, will look to see how her class did on the standardized test on addition and subtraction facts given the previous spring. Based on these standardized test scores, the teacher then divides the class into skill groups. Often this skill-group label, applied in the first grade or even kindergarten, moves through the grades with the child: once a bluebird, always a bluebird. Even if a teacher gives these skill classifications euphemistic titles such as bluebirds and robins, everybody knows there is no hope for the buzzards. Everybody knows the buzzards will review the old "math facts" forever—while the bluebirds move on to new topics.

Parents and teachers pay lip service to the credo that every child is an individual. But they worry about the headlines screaming that American fifth graders do not score as well on worldwide mathematics tests as do their Japanese or French counterparts. Lately, politicians and their statisticians have been pushing hard for a national mathematics test for all fourth graders in the United States. The statisticians want to make sure that all nine-year-olds are right on track, learning what they should be learning so they can come out on top in the world of ten-year-olds.

Some parents and teachers, however, worry about treating children's learning as though it were a determined number of laps at the Indianapolis 500 or a commodity to be graphed along with the Gross National Product. These parents and teachers don't deal with the abstract children of the politicians' pronouncements. They are looking at Julie or Daniel and asking, "Who is this child, what test is going to measure what this child knows, and what curriculum is going to help this child be all he or she can be?" Parents and teachers are even beginning to assert that maybe, just maybe, at age five-and-a-half, Daniel need not be labeled as "immature," especially when that term has become an educational euphemism for "loser."

Many parents and teachers are beginning to suggest what Daniel needs most is some time and space—and a rich environment of educational opportunity. The best thing for Daniel is for us to withhold judgment about whether or not he "measures up" to other kindergartners across the country, and the best thing for Julie may not be a mathematical curriculum designed to make her "look good" in four years when she's compared with ten-year-olds in Korea.

What Should Every Governor Know?

But not everyone agrees. At the National Summit on Mathematics Assessment in April of 1991, people concerned with mathematics education in the United States gathered in Washington, D.C., to figure out what it is that every fourth grader should know. Colorado Governor Roy Romer, chairman of the National Education Goals Panel and a strong advocate of national testing, expressed disbelief and disgust that educators seemed to be hedging on the answer. The conferees were a prestigious gathering: professors of mathematics, the director of Oak Ridge National Laboratory, the executive officer of the National Research Council, the president of Educational Testing Service, the president of the National Council of Teachers of Mathematics, mathematic supervisors from many state departments of education, the U.S. Secretary of Education, and so on. The "Education President," George Bush, made an appearance. To the credit of all present, nobody stepped forward to tell Governor Romer just what it is that every fourth grader in the nation should know. To the discredit of all present, nobody stood up and asked why no fourth grade teachers were present to give their views on the absurdity of the question.

When I brought up Governor Romer's question in Bellevue, Washington, superintendent Don O'Neil countered, "So what does a *governor* need to know? Why not let the fourth grade teacher whip out *that* competency test?"

Close Encounters of the Third Grade Kind

I feel confident in asserting that at least 90 percent of those present at that meeting had not been in close proximity to any fourth graders in a decade or more. Indeed, I'd be surprised to learn that anyone in that audience besides me had ever been shut up for a year in a room with 25 elementary students of any age. And I was invited to that meeting as a reporter, not as a teacher. When national policymakers sit down to decide what to do in education, teachers are not on the guest list.

If teachers are conspicuously absent from such meetings, so are children and researchers who work with children. I didn't hear anyone at the meeting quoting Eleanor Duckworth, a professor at Harvard University and director of the Harvard Teachers' Network who studies how children learn. According to Duckworth, "Any class of children has a great diversity of levels. Tailoring to an average level of development is sure to miss a large proportion of the children."

I wish the functionaries at the National Summit on Mathematics Assessment could meet Marilyn Burns's third graders and learn about the alternative approaches to arithmetic algorithms that she offers them. Rather than emphasizing the mastery of the times tables and the standard algorithm for multiplication, Burns has written a replacement unit that integrates multiplication into other strands of the math curriculum: geometry, probability, statistics, and patterns and functions. "The emphasis of the unit," says Burns, "is to help children develop understanding of multiplication through problem-solving investigations in broad mathematical concepts." Burns focuses on the nonstandardized students rather than the standardized text or test. She documents the work of third graders who very much resemble Daniel and Julie, students of wide-ranging understanding and strategies.

In Burns's model, students of all abilities work on the same problems in an environment of exploration. Students are asked to investigate, theorize, construct, and explain how they reach their conclusions. "Did anyone do it a different way?" is a question frequently asked by Burns. Burns also asks her students to explain in writing their own problem-solving strategy or to explain it a different way. She thus encourages them to "borrow" from the community discussion, to learn from each other. By the time Burns has shown a few more examples of students' work, teachers can see that Josh always comes up with "friendly number" types of problem-solving shortcuts and Maria is still counting by ones. At the end of a three-day training course on this multiplication replacement unit, teachers in northern California applauded Josh, whose strategies they'd come to appreciate. When trying to figure out 6×7, Josh wrote, "I always start with something I know. $6 \times 6 = 36$. Plus one more 6 is 42. Or I could do $7 \times 7 = 49$ and then minus a 7. Or I could use a calculator. Ha. Ha." When the enthusiasm died down, Burns looked at the audience and commented, "We are celebrating the thinking of a third grader, celebrating a child who has done something clever."

Not Throwing Out the Baby with the Bathwater

No one is arguing that it is not useful for children to know the basic algorithms. But these algorithmic operations should not be imposed too early and without the prior environment of exploration and discovery. Walter Denham, the mathematics education manager of the California Department of Education, believes that fifth grade is soon enough for children to learn the multiplication algorithms. And that's why California teachers are being trained in Marilyn Burns's third grade multiplication replacement unit. In addition to trying out the unit with her own third graders, Burns was in constant communication with third grade teachers in San Francisco, Piedmont, and Tucson, who were simultaneously teaching the replacement unit. And good news spreads quickly. I encountered replacement units all across the country even as it was still being written.

Burns says the hard part is not persuading teachers that the material in this replacement unit is exciting for children but convincing them that this is not meant as enrichment or supplementary material. It is difficult for teachers to replace with something entirely different what all the publishers' scope and sequence skill charts and textbooks—and parents' and school board members' and congressmen's exhortations— tell them should be taught in third grade.

Burns points out that in a traditional arithmetic curriculum, teaching multiplication means getting students to learn the times tables and giving them pages of homework in the standard algorithm to practice. Believing that skills other than the times tables are basic to multiplication, Burns addresses the need for "broadening the common definition of school multiplication." She points to such skills as:

- recognizing the variety of situations that call for multiplication;

- identifying appropriate procedures for carrying out needed operations;

- evaluating the reasonableness and accuracy of solutions;

- applying results in appropriate situations.

Burns does not believe in isolating multiplication from other areas of the math curriculum. Instead, she shows teachers how to integrate ideas from geometry, probability, statistics, and patterns and functions. The emphasis of Burns's multiplication unit is, in her words, "to help children develop understanding of multiplication through problem-solving investigations in broad mathematical contexts."

A popular activity in the Burns multiplication unit is candy box research. Burns explains to students that the president of a candy company wants to sell candy in boxes of 6, 12, and 24, and he would like them to investigate all the different rectangular box shapes possible for each number. The rules are that candy comes in only one layer and the box must be rectangular in shape. Students experiment making configurations using 1-inch-square tiles as simulated pieces of candy. As they figure out an array, they replicate it on half-inch grid paper.

Burns starts students out on their candy box research by talking about a sampler box of four candies. Once the students cut the shapes for half-inch grid paper, they also learn to write mathematical notation of 2×2 and 1×4 and label each rectangle, thus constructing geometrical models for multiplication.

Once students become familiar with the methodology, they figure out what rectangular arrangements are possible for many numbers. Then, following Marilyn Burns's belief in the importance of students' communicating their mathematics understanding, they write the president of the candy company a memo explaining what size they recommend—and telling why.

Suzanne Sheard prepares her third graders at Drachman School in Tucson for their candy box research by asking them to think of as many

FAMILY'S OF THREE

Dear Family's of 3,

We think you should buy a box of 15. That way, if each family member ate 1 each night, it would last for 5 nights. However, if you would like to have your candy last longer, we suggest that you buy a candy box with 12 in it. That way, if each family member ate one each night it would for 4 nights. However, if you would like other suggestions, see the multiple chart below.

MULTIPLE×3 CHART

3, 6, 9, 12, 15, 18, 21, 24,
27, 30, 33, 36, 39, 42, 45,
48, 51, 54, 57, 60, 63, 66,
69, 72, 75, 78, 81, 84, 87,
90, 93, 96, 99, 102, 105,
108, 111, 114, 117, 120, 123,
123, 126, 129, 132, 135.

Above: A Tucson third grader discovers multiples of threes and explains her thinking.

Left: A third grader in Tucson shows the geometric properties of the number 12 as he figures out the best design for a candy box.

number combinations as they can. Along one wall students have made big charts of number combinations:

- things that come in threes: wheels on tricycle, triplets

- things that come in fours: paws on bear, rims on car, toes on dog, strings on cello, wings on a butterfly

- things that come in fives: body senses, New Kids on the Block, nickels in a quarter, sticks in a pack of gum

- things that come in sixes: white stripes on the flag, letters in *Tucson*, cokes in a six-pack...

The list continues on through things that come in elevens: players on a football team, candies in a package of Certs. When a student offers the information that his father says, "Eleven is a banker's dozen," it is added to the list.

When Carol Brooks, mathematics specialist and director of Chapter 1 Mathematics for Tucson schools, visits Sheard's third graders, she offers a challenge: "My family has three people in it. What size candy boxes could we share equally?" Students are quick to answer "3, 6, and 12." Brooks asks another question. "If someone gives us a box of 18 candies, how many will each of us get?" Many hands go up, as they do when Brooks asks, "How about 15?" Then Brooks asks the class what they are noticing. Several students answer, "We're counting by three," becoming aware of another important component of multiplication: pattern.

Another Look at How Children Learn

As I visited K–3 Math Project classrooms across the country, I found teachers dismissing the exclusionary notion of high and low math groups and rejecting the notion of different math problems for different children. Instead, they are looking for interesting and challenging problems that allow all children to engage in mathematical thinking, albeit from differing perspectives. Eleanor Duckworth talks about offering a classroom of children—who are bound to possess a variety of intellectual structures—situations in which they "can come to know parts of the world in new ways."

Harvard University researcher and MacArthur Foundation fellow Howard Gardner, who for more than a decade has been looking at the many facets of intelligence, speaks to this same issue of diversity. Gardner and other researchers in Project Spectrum have been attempting to identify and evaluate the broad range of skills exhibited by preschoolers. Instead of observing and rating children according to some preexisting criteria, Gardner's research team observes children as they work and play in their classroom. They look for what the children do spontaneously, while also documenting those skills and attitudes that suggest "lasting connections to particular real-life pursuits valued by American culture": the initiation of ideas, persistence, confidence, introspection, cooperation, and response to frustration. These researchers note that even preschoolers have "working styles," that is, a preferred way of approaching problems. This documentation of children's qualitative responses to learning materials and setting is a radical departure from the traditional statistical approach, the reliance on numbers, and the quantitative tabulation of a child's ability to do column addition, "borrow" from zero, and figure out what happens when Dick and Jane get five oranges.

Gardner's group worries that "the enduring influence of intelligence and achievement testing in American education testifies to its compatibility with Western notions of mind as a static, unitary entity on which individuals can be measured and compared." They conclude that this is an idea that will discourage any attempts at reform. Others disagree, insisting that we don't have enough tests. Governor Romer seemed to be searching for some single entity that tests can provide when he demanded, "Tell me what every fourth grader should know." Whereas Gardner and his colleagues warn that the narrow range of standardized tests don't measure a lot of important skills and abilities, that "children cannot be viewed in isolation from their social, familial, or experiential contexts," Romer is indignant that a nation that can get men to the moon should be able to decide what it is that ten-year-olds need to know.

Teachers in the K–3 Math Project are struggling with these same issues, seeking ways to provide rich profiles of the individual children in their care while at the same time satisfying the public's demand for information on how these individual children measure up to numbers that represent national standards.

The teachers in this project are focusing on what children do, how they go about solving a problem. Rather than laying out a detailed curriculum for the school year before they even meet the children, teachers use their assessment of what happened in the classroom today to inform their teaching strategies and content for tomorrow. In such classrooms, teaching and assessment are of one piece; teachers make assessment a natural part of the school day, not a test that is shipped in by outside experts to be administered once a year and then forgotten.

Instead of just logging the percentage of right answers in their grade books, teachers are examining the children's thinking processes behind the answers. As they look for patterns, for methods of approach, for insights into student behavior that can inform the next lesson, teachers learn that a wrong answer can be a lot more interesting than a right one. To make both right and wrong answers more meaningful, teachers ask their students to write about math, to explain how they get their answers. From kindergarten onward, children are learning that writing and mathematics go together, that an answer is not complete until it is explained.

Teachers talk about the difficulties of maintaining this role of teacher-as-researcher in their classrooms at the same time they are under the gun of political pressure to speed everything up, to respond to the call for standards and standardization, to compete with the Japanese, to teach more and to teach it quicker. Teachers worry about the demand to turn kindergarten into a high-pressure skill zone where children who do not meet the skill requirements fail. They worry about the escalating skills and pressures that children encounter in each succeeding grade, accompanied by the increased threat of failure. Some schools have computer banks of discrete skills to be learned each year—the number may be 68 or 2,847 or 14,272, depending on how far the skills needed for each task are divided atomistic subskills—and how much money the district wants to spend testing students on these hyperminute skills. Teachers worry that when the curriculum is speeded up, the chances are very slim that the Daniels—or the Julies—or the Thomas Edisons and Thomas Watson, Jrs.—will find the time and opportunity to discover who they are and what they are good at.

People who care about what is going on in schools should take a closer look at Daniel and Julie. Teachers worry about the research evidence supporting the contention that Daniel will be better off repeating kindergarten or being transferred to special education and that Julie will benefit from a class for the gifted. But teachers also worry about large amounts of research evidence contradicting this contention, research showing that students learn from each other—and with each other. This evidence supports those who argue that Daniel and Julie are better off being left where they are: in the mainstream. According to this argument, a classroom should not be a hothouse cultivating a uniform species but rather a garden of varied delight. Just as workplaces include people with a wide range of skills and working styles, so too should classrooms.

So What's the Answer?

For teachers like Mary Bacon the traditional school question changes. No longer is the question, "Does Daniel know as much about numbers as Julie?" Neither is the question, "Does Julie know so much about numbers that she needs to be enriched somewhere else?" For these teachers, a better question is: "How can we help both Julie and Daniel build on what they already know, right here and now in this classroom?"

The fact of the matter is that Daniel and Julie are in the same class and their teacher takes the responsibility of finding lessons that can accommodate both of them, lessons in which both children can find success and challenge. We should note that Daniel is pleased with his mathematical investigations and is every bit as eager as Julie to talk about his "mathematics family portrait." And the portraits are well used by the class. Each child teams up with a partner who has the same total number of family members. They discuss the different combinations possible for that number, discovering, for example, that five might be represented by two adults and three children, one adult and four children, three adults and two children, and so on. While talking about number combinations in family size, the children also explore the same concept with manipulative materials, counting plastic cubes, beans and buttons, and Cuisenaire rods (a collection of rectangular rods of ten lengths and ten colors). In short, the children are given a rich environment in which to discover addition, an addition that begins in and is connected to their own lives. And they learn more than addition.

After much discussion of the number combinations they have discovered, the children use the data they have collected to make a class graph of family size. They discover how large is the largest family in the class and how small is the smallest; they figure out how to keep track of the information; they even encounter the word *mean*.

These children's introduction to mathematics is obviously one of social interaction rather than some arbitrary system to be memorized. It is also rigorous, probing for deep mathematical understanding. If Mary Bacon is asked, "What do kindergartners need to know?" she can respond with what they are learning from their family drawings:

- developing concepts of whole number operations;
- seeing math as communication;
- relating their everyday language to mathematical language and symbols;
- collecting, representing, and interpreting data.

A Lesson from Business and Industry

Thomas J. Watson, Sr., the founder of IBM, seemed to feel pretty much the same way about his son Thomas J. Watson, Jr., as the California mother felt about her thumb-sucking child who was denied entrance to kindergarten. And Watson Senior kept his faith and determination, giving his son time and space to grow at his own pace until Watson Junior was nineteen—and twenty and twenty-five. Watson Junior tells the story in *Father, Son & Co.*:

> While my father was achieving phenomenal success at IBM, I barely made it through high school. It took me three schools and six years before I finally graduated at age nineteen.

Watson Junior got into lots of scrapes, but his father, who was pegged the "Thousand-Dollar-a-Day Man" by the newspapers and earned more than even the phenomenally popular Will Rogers, did not respond in the way one might expect from a high-powered executive:

> The difficulties I was having seemed to bring out a warmth and gentleness in my father that were not otherwise obvious. He knew I was drifting, but he never gave up. He was constantly telling me that childhood wasn't the happiest stage of life and that I had much to look forward to. He said, "No matter what happens, it is a time of great change and nobody coasts through it without lots of problems."

Watson Senior admitted to his son, "I wish you were better in school, and I'm sure you do, but at some point, something will catch hold and you are going to be a great man."

Watson Junior's grades did not improve in college, and he credits the largesse of the university dean for his diploma. Watson thinks the dean felt, "This guy is improving a bit. Best give him a diploma and wish him well." People might dismiss this story because when your father has one of the highest annual salaries in the country, then you don't have to worry about grades. But Watson Junior reaches different conclusions. Fifty years later in his autobiography, he realizes that his father gave him the time and space to find out who he was. His father's patience gave him time to discover things about himself:

> Gradually I reached the conclusion that I might do all right if I worked the whole spectrum of things I was reasonably good at, mainly having to do with people.

Acknowledging that his poor school performance worried him, made it hard for him to see his potential, fifty years later he doesn't tell us when he finally memorized his math facts; instead he tells us that he's grateful he had a father and some teachers along the way who allowed him to grow at his own pace.

More Lessons

Teachers swim in a sea of uncertainty every day as they make their classroom decisions, but until recently most had thought that at least mathematics was a haven of precision: one correct answer per problem. And so elementary teachers studying higher mathematics are amazed to discover that mathematical knowledge is not nearly so precise as we might think. Eleanor Duckworth writes persuasively on the topic in *The Having of Wonderful Ideas and Other Essays on Teaching and Learning*, describing the many meetings she has had over a number of years with a group of teachers. As these teachers talk about the learning of their students, they begin to reflect on their own learning too. Through these discussions, the teachers become very good at making sense of what the students in their classrooms are doing. When a child invents a way to do column addition or long division, for example, his teacher takes the time to study and understand his methodology, so she can talk about "his way" and "my way."

Duckworth presents the following problem to the group:

$$1548$$
$$236$$
$$381$$
$$+1682$$

She asks them to look for ways to add these numbers that do not call upon the conventional way of "carrying." The 12 people in the group come up with eight different methods. And the extraordinary thing is that many people in the group "confess" that when they add outside the classroom, they don't carry but use other methods. They use the carrying method only when teaching their students. And they use carrying in the classroom because, after all, that's the way it's supposed to be done. Teachers are shocked to discover they aren't the only ones with secret methods.

Duckworth asks the group what is so special about the way addition is "supposed" to be taught. "Why do we insist on teaching that one way, given that there are so many possible ways?" One teacher comes up with the answer, only half in jest, that the school method of column addition is paper efficient.

The group then talks about the fact that the conventional method is neat and tidy; you put down as few numbers as possible. But as Duckworth observes, for the sake of this neatness, we hide all reason from the students. For the sake of a neat and tidy paper, we defy good pedagogy. Constance Kamii makes essentially the same point in her work. When given the opportunity—the time and space to work on the whole spectrum of things, to figure out what they know—children will invariably add from the left to the right, thus preserving the sense of place value that is lost when they do it the way they're "supposed to" and add from right to left.

One of the remarkable things for teachers involved in the K–3 Math Project is that they get to work with researchers such as Constance Kamii. As one teacher puts it, "I'm not as radical as Kamii, but I'm working on it." By "radical" the teacher is referring to Kamii's dogma: children cannot be *taught* mathematical processes; instead, children can discover and invent these processes in an environment created by the teacher. She states her position in the titles of her books: *Young Children Reinvent Arithmetic* and *Young Children Continue to Reinvent Arithmetic: 2nd Grade*. Operating on a constructivist theory based on Piaget, Kamii stresses that a number is not empirical in nature, that children construct mathematics for themselves rather than internalize it from the environment.

Rather than teaching children how to manipulate algorithms, stresses Kamii, we should allow them to invent their own. In Kamii's words, "Arithmetic is not a body of knowledge that must be taught through social transmission." She insists that arithmetic must be constructed by each child from his own mental action of putting things into relationships, through his own "reflective abstraction." Furthermore, "If the child cannot construct a relationship, then all the explanation in the world will not enable him to understand the teacher's statements." This is why some children simply don't "get it," no matter how many times it is explained. Kamii insists simply that "number concepts cannot be taught."

Our inability to teach number concepts may be the bad news, but it's also the good news—these concepts don't need to be taught.

Chapter

Do You See a Pattern?

In the dramatic opening to *A Mathematician's Apology*, renowned English mathematician G. H. Hardy announces, "A mathematician, like a painter or a poet, is a maker of patterns. If his patterns are more permanent than theirs, it is because they are made with ideas." Harvard professor and MacArthur Foundation fellow Stephen Jay Gould agrees, describing science as "a search for repeated pattern." For the ecologist, Gould points out, this search involves asking questions; he calls ecology an "explanatory science" requiring the use of differential equations, complex statistics, mathematical modeling, and computer simulation—all in search of patterns. Along the same lines, Standard 13 of the NCTM *Standards*, entitled "Patterns and Relationships" and arguably its most popular, states:

> Patterns are everywhere. Children who are encouraged to look for patterns and to express them mathematically begin to understand how mathematics applies to the world in which they live. Identifying and working with a wide variety of patterns help children to develop the ability to classify and organize information. Relating patterns in numbers, geometry, and measurement helps them understand connections among mathematical topics. Such connections foster the kind of mathematical thinking that serves as a foundation for the more abstract ideas studied in later grades.

The NCTM advocates that children become immersed in the search for pattern from their first day of kindergarten. The NCTM publication *Professional Standards for Teaching Mathematics* provides a vignette based on principles established by Mary Baratta-Lorton. It describes how a kindergarten investigation of patterns might look and sound, providing marginal pedagogical commentary to explain what's going on.

> Pat Kowalczyk's kindergarten class enjoys activities involving continuing patterns that have been started using blocks, beads, themselves, and other items. Today Mrs. K, as the children call her, plans on having her class construct patterns using their names. She thinks that this activity will extend the work she has been doing to encourage them to reason and communicate about mathematics with one another. She has prepared a paper with a 5×5 grid of 2-centimeter squares for each student.

At their tables the students fill out the grid, using one square for each letter of their name. When they finish writing their names the first time, they start over and continue until each of the 25 squares contains a letter.

> *Mrs. K:* Select your favorite crayon and color in the squares that contain the first letter of your name.

> Mrs. K walks around the room observing and listening to the students as they work. When Susan wants to know if she should color both the S's in her name, Mrs. K responds with a question, "Are both the first letter in your name?" Susan thinks for a moment and then says, "No, only this one is," and she colors only the first S in Susan. Mrs. K makes a mental note that Susan seems confident in her decisions and does not seek additional confirmation from her. As she continues to walk around, Mrs. K observes that some children seem to understand the activity and work independently, some are actively conferring with others, and some are asking for her to help them. She muses, not for the first time, about what more she could be doing to foster greater self-reliance by her students.

When the students complete their grids, Mrs. K asks the class if they can predict who has the same patterns of colored-in squares on their grids. She tries to phrase the question so as to encourage the students to reason and to communicate their ideas. She notices that she is improving her ability to construct good questions on the spot.

The students quickly guess that the two Jennifers in the class should have the same pattern. Mrs. K asks several students to explain how they can be sure of this without even checking the girls' grids. When she hears Marcus say, "'Cause they have the same name so their papers gotta be the same too," she is really pleased. Calling on him more often really seems to be paying off.

Searching for the next good question, Mrs. K challenges the students to find similar patterns where the students do not have the same first name. After some checking around, the students find that Kent's and Kyle's grids have the same pattern.

Kent: Maybe names that begin with the same letters look the same.

Mrs. K: Is there anyone else whose name begins with the letter K? [Katrina, Kathy, and Kevin all jump up, waving their hands.]

Katrina: But my grid is different from Kent's and Kyle's.

Kathy: But mine is the same as Kevin's.

Mrs. K: Does this fit the rule that the names that begin with the same letter give the same pattern?

Students: No!

Mrs. K looks around, trying to decide on whom to call and tries to remember who has not spoken much today. She remembers that Nikki has not said anything today, although she did complete her grid quickly.

Mrs. K: Nikki, how can we change our rule so that it works?

Nikki: Well, I think it will work if they have the same number of letters and if their name begins with the same letter.

Laura: Mine matches Kathy's, but our first letters are different.

Mrs. K: Let's check it out. [She holds them up to the window, one on top of the other.] Hey, it looks like they do match!

At this point, Dave, Jane, and José put their patterns by Kyle's and Kent's and are surprised that the patterns match. They don't know how to express their finding. Mrs. K is a little surprised that this is hard to explain. Judy says that it has something to do with the length of the name. Short names seem to match with short names but not long names. Finally, Stanley says that the names with the same number of letters will match. Some of the other students question whether he is right. After examining many other examples, they conclude that he is correct.

After school, Mrs. K reflects on the lesson. She writes a few notes in her journal about Marcus, Nikki, and several other students. She also writes down the task so that she can remember it for the future and indicates that she thinks it could be used profitably again. She is impressed with the students' ability to reason. She thinks that letting the students use different-colored crayons to color in the grids may have distracted from the lesson's primary objective. She makes a note to let students pick only one color next time she uses this activity. Although she thinks she is getting better at formulating good questions, she also thinks that she needs to find more ways to encourage students to communicate their ideas with one another and to build on one another's reasoning.

Nobel physicist Richard Feynman recalls being taught about patterns even earlier, quite literally at his father's knee. His father would set up tiles of different colors for the toddler to knock down:

Pretty soon, we're setting them up in a more complicated way: two white tiles and a blue tile, and so on. When my mother saw that she said, "Leave the poor child alone. If he wants to put a blue tile, let him put a blue tile." But my father said, "No, I want to show him what patterns are like and how interesting they are. It's a kind of elementary mathematics."

In his introduction to *On the Shoulders of Giants*, Lynn Steen observes:

What humans do with the language of mathematics is to describe patterns. Mathematics is an exploratory science that seeks to understand every kind of pattern—patterns that occur in nature, patterns invented by the human mind, and even patterns created by other patterns. To grow mathematically, children must be exposed to a rich variety of patterns appropriate to their own lives through which they can see variety, regularity, and interconnections.

From Temecula, California, to Orlando, Florida, to Greenville, Alabama, primary graders use such manipulative materials as Unifix cubes, colored tiles, and plastic links to identify and construct simple patterns, sorting them into two subsets by size, color, or shape. Children identify AB patterns and build them with a variety of materials. They also have plenty of opportunity to hear and sing patterns, to clap and stomp them. Quite noticeably, teachers do not offer extra help to children who are not clapping or stomping in rhythm; in fact, teachers make no effort to "correct" them. In her popular teacher resource *Mathematics Their Way*, Mary Baratta-Lorton stresses that children need time to develop skills without being singled out for having difficulty. Baratta-Lorton reminds teachers, "Keep in mind that children are supposed to evidence skill at the end of this work, not at the start." She also insists that a child doesn't need to understand a pattern before being exposed to a different one. Pattern work is not sequential and in the long run, says Baratta-Lorton, "children benefit from being slightly overwhelmed. Given time, each child sorts out the elements in his or her own way."

Patterns and Connections

There's a famous story about Srinivasa Ramanujan, an unknown clerk unschooled in modern mathematics whose mathematical talent was recognized by G. H. Hardy. The two men shared a fascination with numbers, a "feel" for numbers that almost turned those numbers into living things. When Hardy visited Ramanujan in the hospital, he commented that the taxi's identification number had been rather dull: 1729, or $7 \times 13 \times 19$. Ramanujan disagreed. "No, Hardy," he said, "It's a very interesting number. It is the smallest number expressible as the sum of two cubes in two different ways."

Robert Kanigel, author of *The Man Who Knew Infinity: A Life of the Genius Ramanujan*, offers this explanation:

> Finding numbers that were the sum of one pair of cubes was easy. For example, $2 + 3 = 35$. But could you get to 35 by adding some other pair of cubes? You couldn't. And as you tried the integers one by one, it was the same story. One pair was easy, two pairs never—never, that is, until you reached 1729, which was equal to $12 + 1$, but also $10 + 9$.

How did Ramanujan know? It was no sudden insight. Years before, he had observed this little arithmetic morsel, recorded it in his notebook and, with his trademark intimacy with numbers, remembered it. Mathematicians relish this story for a somewhat different reason: for them, all numbers are fascinating—if you just see the pattern, you can make a connection.

Marian Pelking's first graders in Las Cruces, New Mexico, bring their teddy bears to school to help them with math. Pelking puts 1-foot-

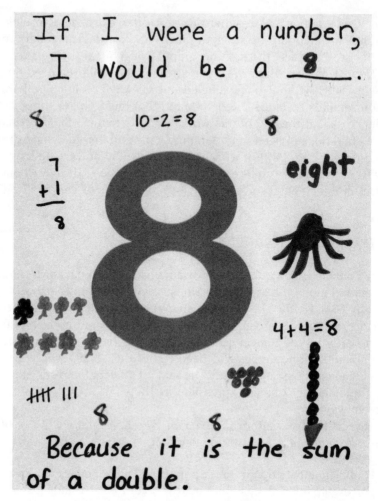

If I were a number, I would be a __8__.

8   10-2=8   8

eight

7
+1
___
8

4+4=8

♣♣♣♣
♣♣♣♣

HHT III   8   8

Because it is the sum of a double.

Kindergartners see the wonderful possibilities in a number.

square tiles on the floor so that her students can construct living graphs. When they go apple picking, for example, they put real apples on their graph. One morning, the children decided to graph their teddy bears according to color. Once all the brown bears and all the white bears were lined up, Pelking asked, "What can we say about these bears?" Jerry replied, "Well, we could say that they're all lined up waiting to get into the bank." Pelking has her eye on this boy: he connects number patterns to real life.

Joan Goodman wrote *Patterns Across New Mexico* for her first and second grade developmental class at the Raymond Gabaldon Elementary School in Las Lunas, New Mexico. To accommodate and enrich a class that is 67 percent Hispanic and about 3 percent Native American, Goodman teaches the unit in both Spanish and English and designs math projects that are culturally diverse.

Goodman's students talk about patterns a lot—describing and drawing the patterns they find on each other's clothing, for example. One child suggests a game: "Let's see who has the most patterns all over him." They write pattern poems and end up producing a class pattern book; they beat patterns on drums, clap patterns, and stomp patterns. They draw Native American patterned pottery in art and incorporate patterns in their hand weavings made of colored yarn and strips of fabric. Using aluminum foil as "silver" plus beads of two colors, Goodman's class puts their knowledge of patterns to good work creating simulated Native American jewelry. Some patterns are simple: ABC, ABC, ABC; others are more complex: AABCCB AABCCB. But every child creates a pattern.

Joan Hammond's first grade classroom in Conecuh County, Alabama, demonstrates that you don't need to rely on a publisher for materials to create patterns in mathematics. Hammond's classroom is filled with a wonderful variety of "things" for children's investigations: locks and keys, nuts and bolts, buttons, even dog tags that were ruined at the manufacturer and then donated to the classroom. It is apparent that this teacher must have "first refusal" on anything in the county before it gets carted to the dump. And children realize the real-world importance of mathematics when materials from their lives are made available inside the classroom.

Third graders in Penny Vincent's class in Albuquerque, New Mexico, are stunned to learn that the patterns they've recognized have helped them solve multiplication without the students even knowing it. Six children working together have the problem of figuring out how many M & M's they have in all when each has two, three, four, and five. David always counts by ones. Keith counts by twos, threes, fours and fives. Sandra makes two groups of six, three groups of six, and three groups of eight. They talk about their strategies, noticing that there are lots of ways to get the same answer. The children are excited when their teacher says that by figuring out faster ways to add numbers together, they are actually multiplying.

Like many teachers who are trying to "humanize" mathematics and connect it to students' lives, Pam Hagler is on the lookout for books with mathematical potential. Hagler reads *How Big Is a Foot?* to her students at the Eugene Field School in Albuquerque. It is a comical story about a king's troubles when he tries to give the queen a bed for her birthday. Beds as we know them haven't been invented yet, and so the king has the queen lie on the floor, wearing her crown (which she sometimes

Above, and on facing page: How Big Is a Foot? by Rolf Myller
provides a literary context for a mathematical principle.

likes to wear to sleep), and he paces off her length—6 feet. Problems
arise, however, because the carpenter's feet aren't nearly so long as the
king's.

When Hagler finishes the story she asks her students, "Did you see
a pattern in the size of the feet and the different beds?" Everybody is
anxious to volunteer but the conversation soon turns to other reactions
the story provokes. When Hagler asks her class if anybody has ever
outgrown a bed, many answers illustrate the sensitivity any teacher
needs, a need exacerbated in an inner city school. Children volunteer, "I
don't sleep in a bed; I sleep on the floor. My brother sleeps in the bed
with my cousin." He continues, "I don't want to sleep there." Several
other students agree that they have a similar situation at their house,
but then Joey warns, "Well, don't sleep on the floor when the heater's
on." Maria chimes in, "If your feet hang out of bed *la cuccaracha* will get
you." Patterns are momentarily forgotten as children make cockroach
jokes, but Hagler regains their attention with an extension of the story,
with teams of students inventing their own units of measurement. Children enthusiastically measure everything in sight and begin an initial
investigation of the relationship to be found between lengths of various
measurement units and the distances measured. There's a parent volun-

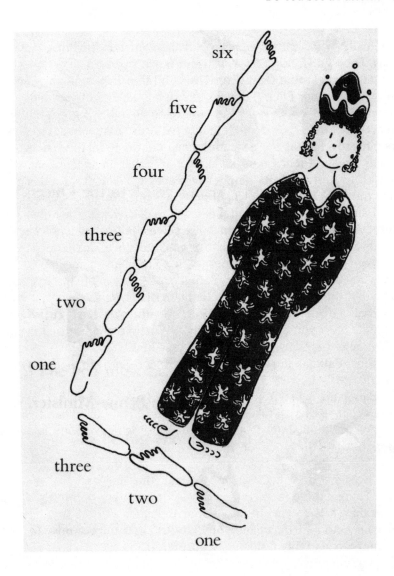

teer in the room helping them measure—a father in a business suit down on his hands and knees admiring the ingenuity of primary graders and getting just as involved in the investigation as they are.

There may be primary classrooms without tubs of pattern blocks, but if there are, I haven't seen them. The collection of six geometric shapes in six colors—green triangles, orange squares, blue parallelograms, tan rhombuses, red trapezoids, and yellow hexagons—are designed so that they can be nested together. Children play with them, explore with them, and eventually work with symmetry, area, perimeter, fractions, and functions. Focused exploration usually starts with patterns.

At the Learning Center for Deaf Children in Framingham, Massachusetts, teacher Ellen Bauman asks seven- and eight-year-olds to use pattern blocks—any blocks they want—to fill in the pattern outlines in an activity book. "See if you find any patterns," Bauman advises. Barry soon discovers that there is more than one way to fill the space. "Three greens always equal a red," he signs. Barry then invents a contest with himself to find the least number of pieces it takes to fill a design and then the most pieces that will fit into the same design.

Bauman leaves Barry and the others to discover on their own. After a while, she interrupts. "Now that you've solved quite a few problems, I want to stop and discuss." Bauman encourages students to talk about what they discovered about different shapes—why some fit and some don't.

They talk about hexagons. Bauman asks how many hexagons it will take to fit the space. "Seven?" volunteers Ginny, her answer half a question, half a declaration. Bauman does not affirm or deny but asks other students, "Do you agree with Ginny?" When someone disagrees, Bauman challenges Ginny, "Can you convince him?"

Next, Bauman introduces trapezoids, and Kathy immediately signs, "There's 20."

Bauman laughs. "You answered before I asked! Would you explain it to us?" Kathy signs, "It takes two pieces for each one, and I had 10 before."

"What's this shape?" asks Bauman and when nobody knows she offers to write the name for them.

"There's 30," says Barry.

"How do you know? Can you explain your answer?"

"There's three in each hexagon. . . . I don't know, but it's 30; I just know that. It just came to me." Bauman pushes a little: "If you had two for everyone and that gave you 20 . . . " Kathy interrupts Bauman's attempts to lead them, signing, "I got 30 too."

Barry jumps up, "There! It must be right." When Bauman presses for an explanation he gives an answer familiar to every teacher: "I just know it." Every teacher knows why when parents ask their children, "What did you learn in school today?" the answer is always "nothing." Children seldom recognize their own intellectual breakthrough or, if they recognize it, they rarely want to talk about it. Children believe they "just know" things.

Kathy and Barry seem to be on the edge of an explanation, don't quite make the intuitive leap, and so fall back on, "It just came to me and I just know it." Bauman respects their struggle and does not "steal" their construction of understanding by spilling the beans, so to speak. She doesn't have a timetable and so she is able to give these children space and time to figure things out.

All this may not look like a profound teaching moment, but it is. In a flash of intuition, sensitivity, and just plain kid savvy, a teacher keeps her mouth shut. All this may not look like multiplication, either, certainly not to a generation reared on memorizing the times tables. Bauman doesn't announce to her students that they are multiplying, but she's definitely getting them ready. It is clear that these children are on the brink of understanding, of creating their own understanding and being able to verbalize it. But while teetering on the brink, they back off, become impatient with putting things into words; they beg Bauman to let them work with the pattern pieces again. They want to figure out more patterns—and do more predicting—without having to explain how they do it. Bauman takes her cue from her students and doesn't push. She agrees with Sheila Tobias, author of *Overcoming Math Anxiety*, who tells us there is a difference between not knowing and not knowing *yet*.

Bauman is pleased with her students' small leap. She smiles and signs her agreement that they should continue their work with patterns—the work they want to do.

Patchwork Quilts and Button Queens

First and second graders in Nancy Litton's class at the Wildwood School in Piedmont, California, engage in a lot of pattern work with quilts. Children are invited to look at quilt books and photographs of quilts. Students choose one quilt to study and then write about the pattern they notice. Using nine 2-inch construction paper squares in two different colors, they create a block of their own quilt patterns, by cutting the squares into triangles by folding on the diagonal.

Litton extends the quilt theme to literature and social studies with such storybook favorites as Patricia Polacco's *The Keeping Quilt*. Polacco, a local author, visits the school, giving children the opportunity to actually see the real keeping quilt. Litton also recommends Sylvia Fair's *The Bedspread*, the story of two elderly sisters who embroider a bedspread that could not be more asymmetrical, a bedspread full of memories and attitudes about how one should live one's life. "It's a book that celebrates individual differences and cooperation," says Litton, who is always looking for opportunities to add value to mathematics by connecting it with literature, art, history, and emotions.

After Litton's students become familiar with quilt patterns and are adept at creating their own, she brings in *Eight Hands Round: A Patch-*

First and second graders in Piedmont, California, explore the pattern possibilities in ninepatch quilts.

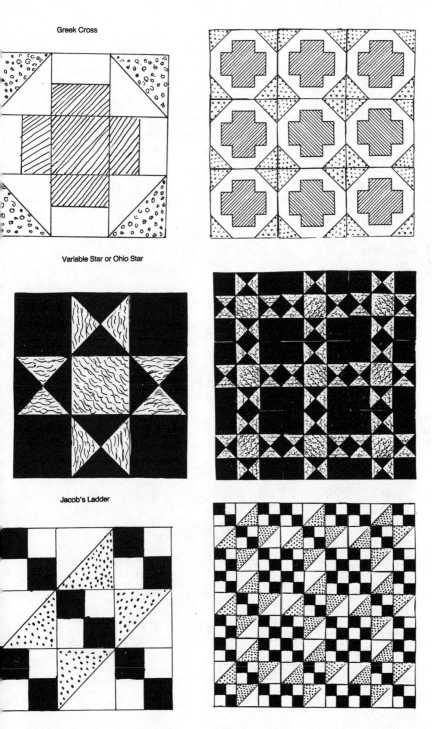

Greek Cross

Variable Star or Ohio Star

Jacob's Ladder

First and second graders in Piedmont, California, study traditional ninepatch patterns.

work Alphabet, an informative alphabet book that speculates on how such early American patchwork patterns as Anvil, Buggy Wheel, Churn Dash, Does and Darts, Eight Hands Round, Flying Geese—on through Yankee Puzzle and Zigzag—got their names. In so doing, it becomes an introduction to metaphor as well as an extension of lessons on symmetry. Litton's students experience a shock of recognition, a flash of Duckworth's "having of wonderful ideas," when they discover that many of the patterns in *Eight Hands Round* are based on nine squares, the structure they've been working with for their own quilt blocks.

Once children see the variety possible with the ninepatch patterns, they form small groups to choose the type of quilt they would like to make. Each group discovers it needs to talk things over before it can actually start work on the quilt. The children need to figure out the shapes that form each of the nine squares in the design. Litton asks them also to take note if

First and second graders in Piedmont, California, collaborate on a quilt.

some of the arrangements are repeated in some of the other squares in the ninepatch. Then they can analyze the individual blocks in the design.

Each group must talk over potential choices. Does each child want to choose his own colors for interpreting his part of the design? Or is this a design that would look best if everyone in the group agreed on the same color for similar parts of the design? Do all the blocks need to be exactly the same? The children must think about not only their own block but also how it will look with all the other blocks that their group produces. Once the preliminary discussion is completed, students begin interpreting the design on 9-by-9-inch grids of white paper. They fold and cut 3-inch squares of colored paper to make the shapes needed to copy the design. Litton lets her students work out their own ways to cut and place the shapes onto the grid. Those who finish first make additional blocks until the group has completed nine blocks.

Once nine blocks have been created, children can make decisions about how to arrange these blocks to form a completed quilt. Litton encourages her students to try out different possibilities, including turning the blocks sideways. Her students are astounded by the dramatic difference this makes in, for example, the Jacob's Ladder pattern. Finally, Litton suggests following up this activity with an opportunity to create an original ninepatch using 2-inch squares on a 6-by-6-inch grid.

Would anyone dare to suggest that these six- and seven-year-olds are not involved in a project of intellectual (and social) rigor, in mathematics that matters?

At the Eugene Field School in Albuquerque, Beth Parker explores line and rotational symmetry in quilts with her fourth and fifth grade combination class. After a quick review of what they know about symmetry, Parker challenges her students to use precut geometric shapes to design quilts that are symmetrical. As her students begin their work, Parker joins a group and works alongside them on her own quilt. Nobody tries to copy the teacher; they are too intent on their own creations. But children notice that the teacher is working on the same project as they are; they notice that she thinks such a project is worth her full concentration. They must notice, as I do, how much she cares about producing a beautiful pattern. Parker's concentration provokes me to reflect on how rarely our students see adults doing mathematics, how rarely our students see us taking mathematics seriously.

As students complete their designs, heated disputes ensue over whether a design is symmetrical or not. Some of the designs are quite sophisticated and the symmetry arguments involve rotating the designs.

What is a fourth and fifth grade teacher doing in the K–3 Math Project? Project director Lois Folsom, obviously proud of Parker's work, explains (sort of), "We tried to follow the guidelines and limit it to K–3, but that doesn't always work." Folsom's grin belies any worry. Likewise, some fourth grade teachers invited themselves into the Montana project. And when budgetary concerns dictated that an Alabama project be limited to K–2 teachers, three third grade teachers invited themselves in anyway.

First graders in Delia Hakim's classroom in Tucson, Arizona, go outside and collect leaves. They talk about what they know already about leaves—and Hakim is not surprised to learn they know a lot already. "I don't start with the premise that students are just waiting to be filled up with my knowledge," she says. "I want them to discover their own knowledge." Students make leaf patterns—they group leaves according to their predominant characteristic: *chiquito, grande, de colores, redonda, orlado, bannan.* "We can read a lot about trees in the textbook—and forget it next week," says Hakim. "Instead, I encourage my students to bring in their own knowledge first—and then to conduct firsthand investigations to learn new things, to figure things out for themselves. We explore our environment first and then read about it in books." Hakim is anxious that her students experience—and enjoy—mathematics as a relevant part of their daily lives.

Hakim points out that, in possession of a collection of wonderful buttons, she was tempted to ask her students to make a graph. Instead, she gave them a more open-ended task, one that would encourage them to create their own learning. Hakim asked, "How could we count buttons?" With such a question, Hakim takes a risk and invites her students to do likewise. She asks them to examine the universe of buttons and figure out a way to exert some sort of control over it. Some children will look at it and see no patterns, no ways to group the buttons. Others will notice patterns: the buttons can be divided into two major groups—white buttons and colored buttons. Other children will notice that buttons have different numbers of holes in them. And so on.

When Patricia Weaver asks her second graders in Tucson, "How many buttons are we wearing today, December 4, 1990?" their predictions range from 51 to 110. Then they begin to talk over how they might find out how many buttons are actually in the room. They come up with these suggestions:

1. Put the children in line and count their buttons.

2. Have each person put a slash mark for every button he's wearing and then add up the slash marks.

3. Have Ms. Brooks (the Tucson math coordinator and frequent visitor to the classroom, who, incidentally, walks in during the button investigation) figure it out.

Brooks agrees that "ask an adult" is definitely a logical and legitimate problem-solving strategy, but she also insists they need to make another choice, one where they aren't getting an adult to do their thinking. As it turns out, Amy is the "Button Queen"; she is wearing 27 buttons. Sundie, Jane, and Julie aren't wearing any. The total number of buttons in this classroom on this day is 90. Finally, the children figure out a way to record their data so visitors can see what they've done.

A primary grader finds a way to report on data collected.

Second graders in Tucson discover what their classmates find scary and report the results.

Their teacher does not hand them a ready-made graph worksheet on which to put their data. Instead, she gives them the time and space to "invent" graphs. And right there on the graph, I see Amy recorded forever as the "Button Queen."

Teachers like Bauman and Hakim and Weaver and Litton are representative of their colleagues across the country. They believe that mathematics is a process of constructing knowledge, not acquiring it. Knowing that patterns are a powerful, unifying force in mathematical understanding, they provide many opportunities for their students to find patterns in the real world. In contrast with encouraging a more deductive approach where students are trained to draw conclusions from "given" ideas that everybody accepts as true, these teachers know that use must precede theory. They place an emphasis on inductive reasoning, encouraging their students to do math, to engage in active mathematical investigation: their students make observations, notice patterns, and then form conclusions.

And so do their teachers. Pattern explorations reveal math's mysteries for teachers, too. When one teacher worked with rectangular arrays in a workshop, she exclaimed, "So that's what square numbers mean?!!!"

The classrooms of project teachers are as varied as the teachers who lead them, but after a year of visits, I have noticed common goals, similar questions that are the foundation of the mathematics curriculum in these classrooms:

1. Do my students see themselves as good mathematicians?

2. Do my students see mathematics as covering a wide range of topics?

3. Are my students developing a flexible repertoire of problem-solving strategies?

4. Are my students able to communicate their problem-solving strategies to others? Can they talk and write about how they solve math problems?

5. Are my students able to assess themselves? Are they able to develop and use criteria to evaluate their performance?

6. Do my students engage in mathematical thinking without a specific assignment? For example, if they have "free time," do they choose math?

7. Are my students developing the attitudes of independent and self-motivated thinkers and problem solvers?

8. Do my students welcome challenges in math? Are they able to focus on math problems of increasing complexity for longer periods of time?

9. Do my students recognize the importance of math in the real world outside school?

10. Do my students use mathematics to solve problems outside math class?

These teachers are not asking what specific math facts fourth graders need to know to please the politicians; they are asking what mathematical insights people need to be useful, creative, and productive participants in a complex world.

Chapter

*Problem Solving
for the
Twenty-first Century*

Students in grades K–8 at the Glen Oaks Park Elementary School in East Baton Rouge, Louisiana, work with teacher Patricia Hale making garbage pizza. In an environmental science project to help students visualize the amount of waste thrown away each year, Hale sends students home to look at their garbage. Then they make cardboard pizzas, depicting percentages of waste in a pie graph: paper gets the largest slice, followed by yard waste, food, metals, glass, and plastics. Students decorate their pizzas with samples of the appropriate trash, so that instead of pepperoni, they have pieces of old newspaper, weeds, M & M's, and so on. These pizzas make a graphic display in the hallway, testimony to students as researchers and problem solvers.

In Las Cruces, New Mexico, when the central office needs to borrow 1000 cubes for a middle school workshop, Marian Pelking's first graders are eager to take on the problem. The children get together in teams and talk over several ways to sort the cubes. The class finally decides to sort by color. Then they count out 1000 cubes by 5s, 10s, and 100s.

For the NCTM, problem solving is the heart of mathematics, and they are talking number sense—garbage pizza and cube-counting shortcuts—

not those nasty little word problems that can be generated by an assembly line of computer technicians who merely substitute "apples" for "oranges" in workbook pages. The NCTM positions problem solving as Standard 1 and gives guidelines specifying that when students engage in problem solving they should investigate and understand the mathematical content in everyday situations, develop strategies to solve a wide variety of problems, and acquire confidence in using mathematics meaningfully.

By placing problem solving at the center of the mathematics curriculum, making it the goal of all mathematics instruction, the NCTM insists that we cannot isolate problem solving and teach it as a distinct subject. The NCTM sees problem solving as a process that must permeate everything that goes on in the mathematics classroom. Problem solving involves estimation and spatial relationships as well as the more traditional word problems. The *Standards* advocate finding problems that help children become thinkers rather than problems that merely rely on memorization of math fact algorithms. Problem-solving strategies include using manipulative materials, finding patterns, making a list or a table. Trial and error is recognized as a legitimate method.

The *Standards* offer the following problem for consideration:

> I have some pennies, nickels, and dimes in my pocket. I put three of the coins in my hand. How much money do you think I have in my hand?

This problem leads children to adopt a trial-and-error strategy. They can also act out the problem by using real coins. Children verify that their answers meet the problem conditions. Follow-up questions can also be posed: "Is it possible for me to have four cents? Eleven cents? Can you list all the possible amounts I can have when I pick three coins?" The last question provides a challenge for older or more mathematically sophisticated children and requires them to make an organized list of possible coin combinations, perhaps like this one:

Pennies	Nickels	Dimes	Total value
0	0	3	30
0	1	2	25
0	2	1	20
0	3	0	15
1	0	2	21

Some Problems Never Go Away

For years, even centuries, problem solving in mathematics has been synonymous with word problems. E. D. Hirsch offers one problem of this sort in his *What Your First Grader Needs to Know*. Hirsch calls it a "math story":

> Kim has 12 sections of orange. She eats 5.
> How many sections of orange does Kim have left?

This kind of word problem, long associated with school arithmetic, has sent shivers of recognition down the spines of children and their parents since the beginning of mathematics itself. It crosses national boundaries and is a popular subject of parody. Some one hundred and fifty years ago, Gustave Flaubert wrote this letter to his sister Carolyn:

> Since you are now studying geometry and trigonometry, I will give you a problem. A ship sails the ocean. It left Boston with a cargo of wool. It grosses 200 tons. It is bound for Le Havre. The mainmast is broken, the cabin boy is on deck, there are 12 passengers aboard, the wind is blowing East-North-East, the clock points to a quarter past three in the afternoon. It is the month of May—How old is the captain?"

A bit more than thirty years ago, a "Talk of the Town" piece in *The New Yorker* offered this word problem:

> You know those terrible arithmetic problems about how many peaches some people buy, and so forth? Well, here's one we like, made up by a third-grader who was asked to think up a problem similar to the ones in his book: "My father is forty-four years old. My dog is eight. If my dog was a human being, he would be fifty-six years old. How old would my father be if he was a dog? How old would my father plus my dog be if they were both human beings?"

More recently, in the summer of 1991, Michael Feldman, host of the National Public Radio program *Wad'ya Know?*, gave his studio audience the opportunity to ask him questions. Feldman approached a smart aleck schoolboy, asking, "Do you have a question?" Without hesitation the boy pounced, "Yes! If a farmer had 16 pigs and he bought seven more . . . " Feldman interrupted, "I'm not in school anymore and I don't have to answer those kinds of questions." The audience clapped vigorously, remembering, no doubt, their own boredom and frustration with the typical school pretense that turning column addition into something called a word problem makes it any more meaningful.

Finding Better Problems

On any given day in K–3 Math Project classrooms across the country, problem solving takes many shapes. Kindergartners in Irvine, California, figure out which color predominates in their Valentine candies: yellow, white, purple, green, pink, or orange. They predict which color they think will appear most often, classify the candies, record their findings, graph the results—and then eat their data. In Belgrade, Montana, the manager of the local IGA store talks math as he makes pizza with every class. Months later, he returns to introduce the math problem that will be the center of the children's attention for the next several hours in the school's Mathematics Olympics: creating a symmetrical design for a new window in his store. This problem requires group planning and collaboration, as well as an understanding of symmetry. Students in Columbia, Missouri, learn about the mathematics of bridge building when professional engineers visit their classroom and help them build a bridge; in Las Cruces, they build a life-size butcher paper replica of George Washington during Presidents' Week. In Albuquerque, Jill Sutterly's first graders tackle this problem:

> Cookies cost 50 cents each. The class sold 27 cookies. How much money did they raise?

Sutterly reports that five first graders are able to solve the problem. Frannie Dever reports that when third graders encounter division on a standardized test, they don't worry that nobody has taught them division; not only do they figure out how to solve the problems, they enjoy figuring out new problems.

In Milwaukee, after Toni Wilson's first graders at Garland School visit the zoo, they decide to investigate the giraffe. They learn that a giraffe can be 18 feet tall. To find out what "18 feet" means, they measure off 18 feet in their classroom with pieces of yarn. Over time, individual children develop a feeling for size by measuring different items in the room with the pieces of yarn. "See if you can find something that's about this long," Wilson challenges them. Children discover that the chalk board and the bulletin board are nearly the same length. There is great excitement when in their reading they discover that a tyrannosaurus rex was also about 18 feet in length. By now, 18 feet means something to them, and they return to the length of the giraffe as a measuring device again and again.

Third graders in math specialist Louise Nielsen's class in Bernalillo, New Mexico, are challenged to use a ruler to make intersecting lines on a sheet of paper. Then they slowly rotate the paper until they can see the Easter Bunny emerge from the field. When a few students complain they can't find the rabbit on the paper, Nielsen replies, "It's hidden. Keep looking." All sorts of rabbits emerge: fat, skinny, and in-between. And students learn that mathematics problem solving involves spatial relationships—and whimsy—as well as computation.

Teachers try to find problems that help students work on basic math in a variety of ways. Early in the school year, Nancy Pender, first grade teacher and math specialist at Shenandoah Elementary School in Orlando, Florida, tells her students, "Let's see how many Link-Its [1-by-1-inch plastic links that come in four colors and easily join together] you can put together in a minute." She tells her students to record their observations in their math journals, including how their individual chains compare with those made by others in their group. Joy writes: "I have 9. Stacie has 7. I have 2 more." Marc's journal entry is shown on page 64.

Later in the year Pender asks students to record in their math journals "What I learned this morning." Michael's schematic summary of how he solved a problem with attribute blocks is shown below.

A set of attribute blocks has four attributes: shape, color, size, and thickness. There are five shapes (rectangle, square, circle, equilateral triangle, and isosceles right triangle), three colors, two sizes, and two thicknesses. Michael uses the attributes of equilateral triangle and redness. He uses squiggly lines to represent objects that fit in neither category.

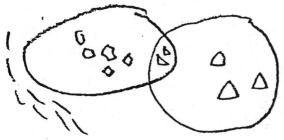

A first grader in Orlando, Florida, uses a Venn diagram to represent attributes.

A first grader in Orlando, Florida, records his observations in his mathematics journal.

Thais Noble's first graders in Las Cruces are also working with Venn diagrams, using a diagram to record their survey of student preferences for hamburgers or hot dogs (shown at the top of page 65).

5 friends like hamburgers.
3 friends like hot dogs.
9 friends like both.

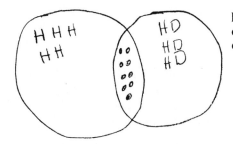

First graders in Orlando use a Venn diagram to record the class's hot dog and hamburger preferences.

Not Apples and Oranges but Half-Pecks of Wheat and Raccoon Feet

Inspired by the NCTM *Standards*, project teachers around the country are looking for a variety of problem-solving contexts. Karen Valdes's first graders at the Vail School in the Temecula Valley School District, California, work with word problems in the familiar format, but since they are studying Eskimos in social studies, that context is brought into their math:

> There are 2 kayaks. 5 Inuits are in each one.
> How many Inuits all together?

and

> There are 3 sleds. Each sled had 4 sled dogs pulling it. How many sled dogs all together?

Such problems offer opportunities for more strategies than the common apples and oranges problem. Children come up with a variety of strategies for solving a multiplication problem without exposure to the traditional algorithm.

After kindergartners in Teresa Mason's class in Las Cruces weigh their potatoes and record the data, they also write about their favorite way to eat potatoes. "We don't do drill, and we don't do dittos," remarks Mason, "but parents are amazed that these children can count by 5s and 10s and they know that this is the 121st day of school and that's an odd number." Patty King's first and second grade combination class in Albuquerque solves problems throughout the day: "How many tables do we need for lunch? How can we figure that out?"

In Orlando, Marsha Copenhaver's kindergartners also solve lunch-time problems: "If five students brought their lunch today, how many hot lunches do we need to order?" Brenda Sample tells her third graders in Columbia, "The answer is 18. What's my question?" and her students come up with many ways to end up with 18. Outside the main office at the Goodwood Elementary School in East Baton Rouge, the week's math problem is posted: "How long will it take Mrs. Sykes [P. E. teacher] to run one mile?" This problem is the submission of a second grader, and everyone in the school from kindergartners to custodians is welcome to submit an answer. Actually, anyone in the community can try: the mail carrier has been known to win the school's problem of the week. Sometimes the community is brought in to help solve the problem. When the puzzler was to figure out the height of the school flagpole, the professional advice of a university professor was solicited. Photographs are taken of first, second, and third place winners, and a set of tangrams is one of the popular, math-oriented prizes.

Because Tyner, Kentucky, is a rural community, and its K–3 Math Project is designed to take advantage of local resources and needs, problem-solving activities often involve gardening and farming. The county extension agent visits second and third graders, teaching them to "step off" a half acre. Children compare pecks of corn to pecks of wheat and see that equal volumes are not necessarily equal in weight. Unifix cubes become handy tools for solving garden plot problems. Children are asked, for example, to figure out the largest area they can enclose with a fence 16 units long. Then they find how many bean plants will fit on that plot if the plants have to be spaced three units apart.

As Judy Sizemore, coordinator of the Appalachian Communities for Children programs and the person responsible for the day-to-day implementation of the K–3 Math Project for the Jackson County School District, points out, such farming and gardening activities "help parents as well as children realize that problem solving in math is more important in their daily lives than they realized."

Students at the Martha Fox Heck School in Belgrade come from a middle to lower socioeconomic farming and agricultural community, and math specialists Earlene Hemmer and Terri Goyins bring the children's world into problem solving. They give their first graders this problem:

Four raccoons went down to a lake for a drink of water.
Two raccoons got their front feet wet and one raccoon got its back feet wet. How many dry feet were there?

The children demonstrate a range of problem-solving strategies in their approach to this problem. As Goyins notes, "They bring themselves too." Teachers see patterns of response over time. Some children take pleasure in giving meticulous attention to every possibility a problem offers—down to filling in every detail of each raccoon's tail, for example. For these children, the process of working through the problem is much more interesting than the answer. Other children are more impatient. Eager to get to the answer, they reduce the elements to a sort of shorthand abstraction—something that's on the page only as a reference to be counted.

Jeff carefully draws all the raccoon feet; then he goes back and puts an X on all the wet ones. Once that is done, he can go back and count all the legs without an X.

Anna uses the same method, abstracting the feet forms into loops and marking the wet ones with an X.

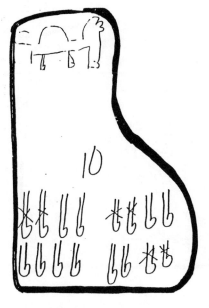

Left: Jeff marks the wet raccoon feet with Xs.

Right: Anna's raccoon feet are also marked with Xs.

Left: Alyssa puts dots for dry feet and rectangles for wet ones.

Right: Craig introduces standard mathematical notation.

Alyssa's methodology is similar to Anna's but with a significant alteration. Alyssa explains her basic thinking: "I got my aksr buy pootyR dots four thare feeb. [I got my answer by putting dots for their feet.]"

What Alyssa doesn't mention in her explanation is that she streamlined her problem-solving methodology by putting dots for the dry feet and rectangles for the wet ones.

Craig also explains his thinking: "I counted with my fingers," and he introduces standard notation: 8 − 4 = 4.

Top: Lucy draws the raccoons but does not come up with an answer.
Bottom: Maryann colors the wet feet so she can more easily count the dry ones.

Lucy draws the whole raccoon and begins to label each pair of legs. She seems to run out of steam and does not come up with a solution. Maryann also draws the whole raccoon, coloring the wet feet solid black so she can easily go back and count the dry ones.

Left: Marybeth concentrates on drawing raccoons but does not get an answer. *Middle:* One of Daniel's raccoons is spread-eagled—to keep those feet dry. *Right:* Paul's first raccoon stands on his head to keep those back feet out of the water.

With careful attention to detail, Paul, Marybeth, and Daniel all draw the raccoons in or near the water. Paul's first raccoon stands on its head to keep those back feet out of the water. Similarly, one of Daniel's raccoons is spread-eagled to keep two feet dry.

These children's teachers do not pose a problem so they can log right and wrong answers in their grade books; instead, they are looking for problems that will enable students of varying abilities to invent a variety of strategies for solving the problem; they are looking for insights into how children approach a problem, helping them to structure their own teaching. They are using the children's work to inform the lessons they will present tomorrow. As they watch these children throughout the year Hemmer and Goyins note how personality influences mathematics. Before long, they can predict that Jeff will be meticulous in his depiction of detail, always giving a problem a kind of personality; Alyssa always streamlines, always moves to the abstract. Hemmer and Goyins look for problems that will encourage a range of strategies, offering children many ways to be "right."

Another Way

At the Learning Center for Deaf Children in Framingham, Massachusetts, when Ellen Bauman asks eight-year-olds to use pattern blocks (a set of blocks containing six geometric shapes in six colors) to fill in a picture, Billy immediately asks, "Can I have eight parallelograms for the giraffe?" Bauman asks, "Why do you want eight?" and Billy shrugs and replies, "I don't know yet—I just want to see if eight works." Bauman is comfortable with Billy's reply. At some point she might even comment, "Trial and error can be a useful problem-solving strategy," but for now she just nods and signs, "OK!" After Billy and the others in his group fill the space one way, they don't stop but immediately start looking for other ways to fill the same space. At age eight, their experience in this math class has shown them that many mathematics problems have more than one solution.

"I *will* be finished," Billy signs to his teacher, his grin indicating that he's not anxious to be done with problem solving.

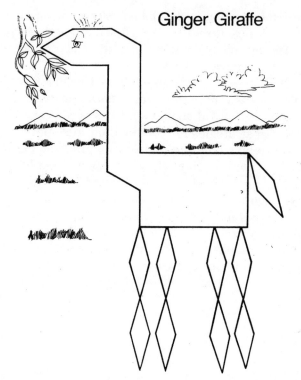

Ginger Giraffe

Children use pattern blocks to explore geometrical relationships.
(Courtesy Cuisenaire Company)

Pumpkin Juice and Pumpkin Math

Chris Confer, instructional support teacher for math at the Ochoa Elementary School in Tucson, Arizona, teams up with Delia Hakim to explore pumpkins with Hakim's first graders. First Hakim asks the children to share everything they know about pumpkins. After much discussion of cutting jack o' lanterns, the students begin to explore size and texture. One child thinks there will be seventy seeds inside; another is sure there must be a million. "What is always inside a pumpkin?" she asks. The children agree that there are seeds and meat and juice inside. The teachers admit to being rather surprised about the juice. The children talk about the parts of pumpkins. "The stem is so I can hold on to it; the button on the bottom is to hold the seeds and the juice in." The children put the pumpkins in order, biggest to smallest.

Confer notes that asking children, "What pumpkin activities would you like to do?" only gives rise to a school-type activity the children had done before: carving a jack o' lantern. But after watching the children explore and listening to them talk, she and Hakim zero in on some concepts that seem to be more important than others. For instance, size and weight comes up over and over. Confer notes that as she writes up a lesson plan for the next day, it is full of "ifs" and "mights." In her words, "Not only are our units of study impossible to plan ahead, but even the daily lesson plans are merely possibilities." She and Hakim decide they might ask each child to cut a string to predict the circumference of a pumpkin and then sort their strings into categories of "too long," "too short," or "just right." They like the idea but they know that if something else comes up, they are both comfortable with dropping this, changing their plans and winging it.

Hakim starts the next day by placing the pumpkins on the rug in random order, but quickly the children rank them by size. And they give the pumpkins names: *papa, mama, tio, tia, nina,* and *bebe.*

The children begin talking about the fact that the pumpkins are all different colors. "Arturo's pumpkin is yellow."

"How do you know that one is Arturo's pumpkin?" asks Hakim. "His is the biggest one."

"What is big?" asks Confer. "What does *big* mean?"

"Fat."

"How big around is Arturo's pumpkin?" asks Confer. "Do you think you could cut a string that would go around the middle of Arturo's pumpkin?" The children are sure they can and they do it. Confer introduces the word *circumference,* and the children like the word and use it. Confer describes what happens next:

> When the children had the opportunity to try to fit their string around Arturo's pumpkin to verify their predictions, they were transfixed. Silence filled the room. Eyes and mouths were open wide as they watched the first child. She stretched her string around the pumpkin's middle. "Oh!" gasped the children as they saw it fall short of its mark. All eyes watched her tape her string to the chart in the section labeled "too short." And even though these first graders had been working nearly an hour, this kind of attention continued as each child took his turn. This was "on-task" of the finest kind.

Confer continues:

> The children took control of the activity. They recorded. They decided who would go next. And the "too short" section grew fuller and fuller. Soon, as the sections had no dividing lines, it was hard to

tell if a particular string was "too short" or "too long." Christian noticed and solved the problem by drawing a wobbly line down between the sections. As the last few children awaited their turns I noticed some furtive behavior that was trying to tell us teachers something: the waiting children were using their strings to measure things near them. Felipe, for example, quietly held his string taut against a book, against the leg of the chair, against his foot.

Confer asks Felipe to explain what he is doing and then everybody wants to do likewise. So the teachers cut a circumference string for each pair of children, and they find things to measure, recording their findings on a "shorter, longer, same length" chart. In teacher jargon this is known as an extension activity. It isn't in the planbook but is the result of teachers watching children and adjusting the lesson to meet their interests and needs.

Cows and Chickens

Across the country, one problem has become an instant classic, appearing over and over, both in its original form and in regional transformations. The "cows and chickens problem" comes from *A Collection of Math Lessons from Grades 1 through 3* by Marilyn Burns and Bonnie Tank. Here's how they do it:

"I'm going to tell you a story," I told the class of first graders, thus beginning the lesson. "Listen carefully, because there is a problem for you to think about in this story." I presented the situation to the children. "I took a ride in the country last weekend and drove past many farms," I told the class. "At one farm, I noticed a farmer standing near the road, looking up at a hill in the distance. He looked very worried. I stopped my car and got out."

"Is something wrong?" I asked the farmer.

"Yes," he answered, "I have a problem that I need to solve. I have one field up on that hill there." He pointed at the hill. "There are four cows and three chickens in the field. I know that because I put them there. Also, there is a fence around the field. What I'm wondering is how many feet and tails they have altogether. I'm trying to figure that out without climbing up the hill to the field to count."

"I told the farmer that I knew a class of children who were learning about solving problems, and I thought the class could figure this out. I'm going to give you a chance to solve the farmer's problem."

I wrote some of the information on the board. This gave me a chance to review the story.

There are 4 cows.

There are 3 chickens.

How many feet and tails are there altogether?

I explained to the children how I wanted them to work. "You won't work alone on this problem," I told the children. "You'll each work with a partner. You and your partner will have one piece of paper for both of you to use together.

"Here is what you and your partner are to do," I continued. "First you need to tell each other what the problem is so that you're sure you both understand it. Then, before starting to write anything on your one piece of paper, you need to talk about what you will put on the paper and how you will share the work."

Five pairs of children come up with the right answer. Other answers range from 20 to 34. Significantly, all the students seem satisfied with their results; none worry over the reported discrepancies and none ask which answer was the right one. The children do ask, however, if Burns is going to take their papers to the farmer.

For second graders, Burns ups the ante a bit, asking children to figure out how many feet and tails there are for five cows and four chickens. On their own, these students write letters of advice to the farmer.

Mississippi River Math

Catherine Stephens, math specialist and assistant principal at the Audubon Elementary School in East Baton Rouge, helps third graders write problems that draw on their own unique locale. The students collect some of their problems about swamps and crawfish and the Mississippi River into a book. Then, typing their own problems using a computer, the students make a version for Stephens to display at her presentation at the 1991 NCTM conference in New Orleans. Stephens throws an autograph party to celebrate the book's publication.

Three Baton Rouge third graders write word problems with a Louisiana flavor (*shown above and on pp. 77-78*).

ickolas Reynolds.   Property in th Marsh

Bayou Billy owns $\frac{3}{8}$ of a marsh, John Doe owns $\frac{8}{24}$ of the same marsh, the Louisiana government owns the rest of the marsh, How much of the marsh does the government own?

Catching Crawfish

If crawfish catchers caught 883 crawfish and gave them to Brunets Restaraunt and they Sold them to 350 people who bought two each, how many were not taken?

BONUS: Each crawfish cost $1.75, how much money did they make?

BONUS

$$350 \times 2 = 700$$

$$-7 \quad 883 - 700 = 183$$

$$\$1.75 \times 2 = \$3.50$$

$$\$3.50 \times 350$$

$$000$$

$$+ 1750$$

$$1050$$

$$\$1225.00$$

By, Jennifer Erin Hayden

Just as children vary widely, so too does the degree of computational difficulty in the word problems they write. Because they do not regard this book project as competitive, they all take pride in the unique touches they are able to bring to their individual problems. And, since the children are aware that the Exxon Education Foundation helps their teachers make many special projects in math possible, Ryan decides to give Exxon its own problem (see page 80).

Math Has Changed and So Have Those Word Problems

Milwaukee Public Schools teach "from a problem-solving perspective within a Cognitively Guided Instruction (CGI) framework," meaning that teachers use word problems to teach addition and subtraction from the very first day of school.

Professor Jean Moon, Exxon project director at the Center for Math and Science Education Research, University of Wisconsin, Milwaukee, points out that the most interesting part of CGI is not the problem but the student explanation. "Teachers are zeroing in on student strategies rather than just checking that the answer is right; they are encouraging students to share their strategies with each other. When a student explains a strategy, the teacher doesn't say 'right' or 'wrong'; she asks, 'Did anyone use a different strategy?' Students learn there is more than one way to solve a problem."

Mathematics thereby becomes something that students create rather than a finished product that is transmitted to them by the teacher or the text. Teachers emphasize counting strategies embedded in word problems rather than math facts. Such methodology builds on the premise that students come to school already possessing numerous strategies for solving addition and subtraction problems. By minimizing the introduction of disembodied "facts," teachers encourage students to use the strategies they already possess; this means that teachers also accept and encourage many different strategies for solving a problem.

Milwaukee students are very familiar with the CGI framework and expect their numbers to be in a problem-solving context, as is revealed in this story shared at one of the regular Saturday morning math meetings organized by Moon and available for university credit: A first grade

EXXON'S Problem

There was some Exxon Employees and they were wondering how much could they spend on each gas and oil storage tank. They have 23 tanks and they have to pay an equal amount of money on each tank. Each tank had to have $5,630 Dollars on it... What will they be spending on all the tanks.

$5,630
× 23
16890
11260
133490

petro   oil
GAS
NATURL GAS

The factors are 5,630 ₵ 23
The product is 133,490

Ryan
Brown

A Baton Rouge third grader writes a word problem for Exxon.

teacher standing at the bus stop with her students asks, "What's 5 + 5?" Her students respond, "What's the problem? Who has five what?" Similarly, when I ask Rasheedah, a first grader at the Garfield School, what she's doing, she puffs up and proclaims, "I'm doing math!!" Then I ask, "Can you make a story?" Before she answers, Rasheedah asks me my name. I tell her, "Mrs. O," and Rasheedah smiles. "O.K. Mrs. O had nine Popsicles. I took four away from her and then Mrs. O had five left."

Daquanda joins us with her story. "Brett had seven baby gerbils. And they're right here!" The story problem extends into the classroom around us as we go admire the gerbils. The children continue the real life story problem: "We had seven gerbils. Then we had six more. And that's 13. Because 7 + 6 = 13."

Other children chime in, "I know 100 − 1; I know 80 + 3." These children are proud of their math ability and eager to share what they know.

Amelia Rodriguez, a first grader at the Allen Field Elementary School in Milwaukee, invents a problem that is far more sophisticated. It is, in fact, akin to the Burns and Tank cows and chickens problem and the Montana raccoons: "Santa has eight reindeer; each reindeer has four legs. How many legs are there all together?"

Members of Amelia's group come up with a variety of strategies to solve her problem and their individual strategies provide insight into their mathematics capabilities for their teacher, Marlene Gowecki. Donald, for example, uses Multilink cubes (interlocking plastic cubes) to represent the legs physically—outlining their shape. Donald has eight groups of four legs, but since he has used four cubes to represent each

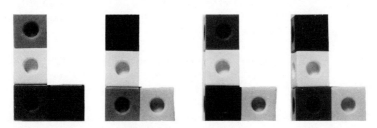

A Milwaukee first grader uses Multilink cubes to figure out how many candies are in four Christmas stockings.

leg, he comes up with a very large total. Gowecki notes that even more revealing than his inability to make symbolic abstractions of the reindeer leg is the fact that Donald cannot count accurately the cubes he has laid out. He counts some twice while missing others. The children are intent on setting up and solving the problem and explaining their strategies. Nobody questions the discrepancies; nobody asks who's "right."

Gowecki tells another group, "There are four stockings hanging on Christmas Eve, with three candies in each. Show me with cubes how you're going to figure out how many candies there are." Joey lays out five groups of three; Mike carefully makes three stocking shapes out of his cubes. You might suppose that Mike comes up with the wrong answer, but he doesn't. The three cubes on the left side of each stocking represent the candies. The cube on the right represents the stocking. So, as Mike explains to his group: "3 + 3 + 3 + 3 = 12."

After working with her cubes, Anna reports, "There are 12." Not taking anything for granted, Gowecki asks, "Twelve what?"

"Twelve stockings," replies Anna, proving that a teacher can't rely on "right" answers as evidence of student understanding.

I am reminded of Charles Dickens's *Dombey and Son*, which was first published in 1854. When Paul Dombey's teacher says that, eight being the highest number, he finds Dombey at six and three-fourths, Dombey doesn't know how to take it.

> Being undecided whether six three-fourths meant six pounds fifteen, or sixpence three farthings, or six foot three, or three-quarters past six, or six somethings that he hadn't learned yet. . . .

Gowecki does not move in and tell some students that they are right and others that they are wrong. She knows that all students understand math at some level, and she tries to build on their individual understanding. She thus creates an environment in which children are willing to take risks, one that provides plenty of opportunity for her to make continual informal assessment, planning future lessons from her observations.

Examining One's Craft

The Fifty-Fifth Street School in Milwaukee is a Spanish immersion school. Children are chosen by lottery, and the staff speaks Spanish from the very first day. In Susan Walters's second grade, students sometimes answer in English, but Walters speaks only Spanish when she poses problems. "Debra had nine boxes. She gave some to Tony. Now she has three boxes left. How many boxes did Debra give to Tony?" The emphasis is not on the answer but on how they got it. Walters always asks for their strategy. She always asks, "Did anyone figure it out a different way?"

In their monthly Saturday meetings, Jean Moon and Milwaukee teachers work on observable criteria for assessing this kind of problem solving. They look beyond the answers, giving weight to student volunteering, enthusiasm, and conferring with each other, as well as the more traditional criteria such as verifying and explaining the problem.

Pat Cassady, director of the primary math program and project head for the K–3 Math Project in Conecuh County, Alabama, credits a student with refining her assessment criteria. "She taught me about the fact that when numbers mean nothing to students, they rely on teachers' body language and other clues":

I asked, "Corrine, what answer did you get?"

"Seven."

"Will you please explain why?"

"No, I mean eight."

"Corrine, why did you change your mind?"

"Since you asked me another question, I figured my first answer must be wrong."

Cassady explains this was one of those profound moments of awakening: "That's what happens when students are never asked to explain their answers. Corrine's reply will ever be with me when I ask students to talk about their work." Cassady reflects that somehow we build a system where many students are far more worried about pleasing the teacher—and psyching her out—than thinking about the problem.

Cassady, now a high school teacher, observes, "If my students have a worksheet that has an estimate column and an actual column, they will get the answer with the calculator—say, 42.17—and they'll put 42.16 as their 'estimate.' They aren't cheating; they are trying to please the teacher. If the teacher wants them to be good estimators, then they'll be really good estimators—only 1/100 off." Cassady concludes, "If you drill it into students' heads that there is only one answer, if you say their future depends on standardized test scores, then how can you expect them to get to tenth grade and take a risk and start making good guesses?"

Marian Pelking, first grade teacher and math specialist at East Picacho Elementary School in Las Cruces, hopes her students will be very comfortable with estimation and risk-taking by the time they reach tenth grade. She likes estimation activities because they help children to develop number sense, a feeling for what makes a good guess different from a bad guess, and she is confident that, over time, a lot of such guessing will help children become risk-takers. Pelking helps her students learn, "You can be wrong and still have made a good guess."

Pelking began to suspect, however, that perhaps she had asked for estimates too regularly when she got this response to a classroom problem:

> I was going to do a science demonstration and I wanted the children to be aware that when ice melts, you don't seem to have as much left as when it was solid. I showed them two pitchers filled with crushed ice and asked, "What do you think we're going to do?"

> "You're going to make us estimate how many pieces of ice," sighed Jean, "and then you're going to make us count them." Deeper sigh accompanied by whole class groans.

Pelking laughs. "I guess I'm telling a story on myself. But it taught me something. I will lay off asking them to estimate everything in sight." But even as she laughs at herself, Pelking also recognizes this as a story of triumph. Three or four years ago one of her first graders wouldn't have even known the concept of estimation, never mind the terminology—or the number sense, the developing savvy for large and small amounts.

It's Not What I Say . . .

Sometimes teachers realize that they don't always practice what they preach. Math specialists attending a monthly meeting in East Baton Rouge find the tables turned when they are given a problem to solve in estimation:

> You will have three tries to guess the number of cubes in the Coke bottle. After each guess you will be told if your guess was too high or too low. If one person at your table guesses the correct number, everyone at your table will win a prize. Good luck!

A timeline is provided for the three guesses, the first guess is due soon after the meeting assembles. There are six people at each table and they get to work calculating their individual guesses so they can hand them in at the appointed time. Everyone does her own work, keeps her eye on her own paper. There is no discussion. But once each group gets back notification of "too low" or "too high," a murmur starts up around the room. People reread the directions to each other: "If one person at your table guesses the correct number, everyone at your table will win a prize." Teachers realize their table has a much better chance to win if they collaborate. They moan about wasting their first round of guesses. As one teacher observes, "We tell our students to collaborate, but we had to learn it the hard way for ourselves."

In a *New Yorker* article of December 17, 1990, MacArthur Foundation fellow and photographer Richard Benson talks about teaching. "There's a terrible problem I run into in teaching, which is that when you tell people something, you keep them from ever knowing it. If they find it on their own, they'll know it in a way they never will if you tell them. What I try to do more and more is to bring my students up here to my studio and get them really working." Ginny Bolen, project director for the K–3 Math Project and supervisor of mathematics for the East Baton Rouge School District, agrees with Benson, and she extends the importance of a hands-on discovery method to teachers. "Teachers learned more about collaboration in that brief experience of self-discovery through the estimation contest than they would receive from half a dozen lectures."

What's Wrong with Memorizing the Times Tables?

In some schools mathematics does look very different these days, and a lot of otherwise cordial people are not happy. When teachers at the thirty-sixth annual convention of the International Reading Association in Las Vegas asked prize-winning children's book author and illustrator Allen Say what he thought of American education, he answered in two words: "It stinks." The story he told to illustrate his point is one very familiar to any primary teacher who teaches mathematics. Say told his audience that just a year go, when his daughter was in fourth grade, he discovered she didn't know her times tables:

> My god! I was appalled. I went to see her teacher. The teacher told me, "Mr. Say, we don't believe in feeding our kids a bunch of facts."
> I asked, "What's wrong with memorizing the alphabet? What's wrong with memorizing your telephone number? Your address?"

The teacher said, "It's a different thing, Mr. Say."

So I said, "All right, if my daughter doesn't know how to do her times tables, how do you expect her to do more complicated calculations?" The teacher looked at me as if I were mad. She said, "We let them use calculators."

Say recalls that he was "too stunned even to argue with the teacher. I went home. I decided to take this matter into my own hands. I drew up the times tables sheet. I told my daughter, 'If you memorize this by the end of this week, I will give you 10 bucks.' She immediately went to her room. About an hour and a half later she came back out. She knew the times tables backwards, forwards. It cost me $10."

There are several morals one can draw from this story:

- A lot of intelligent people believe the ability to do complicated reading and mathematics rests on first memorizing a discrete series of skills. These skills are represented by the alphabet and math facts.

- When all else fails in getting kids to recite basic facts, bribes will do the trick quickly and effectively.

- Teachers need to do a better job in communicating the purpose and philosophy of their academic programs to parents, particularly when sacred rituals are involved. Announcing that times have changed will not substitute for an explanation.

- If schools don't apply too much pressure about basic fact memorization too early, the kids can learn those facts in about an hour and a half when they are ready.

A short news article from *The New York Times* of April 4, 1931, giving the results of a city-wide arithmetic test for elementary students, demonstrates how times have indeed changed. No general average of achievement in the test was announced, but the results were said to have shown citywide averages as follows:

12.4 examples in addition correct in 8 minutes working time; 12.2 examples of subtraction correct in 3 minutes working time; 2.8 multiplication examples correct in 5 minutes; 1.3 examples in division correct in 8 minutes.

So the math of the 1930s is straightforward arithmetic: basic algorithms. The problems themselves are not considered newsworthy—just the speed at which they are solved.

In contrast, Philip Hilts tells the story of a physicist using simple mathematics for real-world problem solving. Dr. Robert Wilson, a particle physicist who was the director of Fermilab from its inception in 1967 until 1978, was in on every detail of Fermilab's design, including the price of dishes. As Hilts tells it:

> The plans for the Fermilab cafeteria called for a freight elevator to move all the dishes from the dining area to the kitchen. When Wilson found out what the cost of the elevator was, he thought it outrageously high. He quickly called up the cafeteria manager. "How much does a place setting cost? How many meals would you serve in a year?" When he hung up the phone he flatly told the architect: "Forget the elevator. Build me a chute from the cafeteria straight into the Dempsey Dumpster. We can get twenty years of dishes for the price of one elevator!"

Wouldn't you like to meet his third grade teacher?

Yes, mathematics has changed: these days we have calculators for speed; now we're looking for problem solvers who can figure out when it's better to buy dishes than build elevators.

Chapter

4

Arithmetic:
Adventure or Algorithm?

Marilyn Burns offered mathematical adventure to a packed ballroom at the 1991 annual convention of the National Council of Teachers of Mathematics in New Orleans. Drawing on Laura Geringer's picture book *The Three Hat Day* (Harper, 1985; Trophy, 1987; illus. Arnold Lobel), Burns read to the audience that:

> *R. R. Pottle the third loved hats.*
> *He loved fur hats*
> *and firemen's helmets*
> *and felt hats with feathers*
> *tucked in the bands.*
> *He loved top hats*
> *and tiny hats.*
> *He loved silk hats*
> *and straw hats*
> *and sailor hats.*
> *He loved berets*
> *and bonnets*
> *and bathing caps*
> *and bowlers.*

R. R. Pottle walks down the street wearing a bathing cap, a fireman's hat, and a sailor's hat. Burns invited each person in the audience to talk with a neighbor about how many different ways R. R. Pottle can wear, simultaneously, the bathing cap, fireman's hat, and sailor's hat.

When she called on a teacher in the audience for an answer, he replied, "He can wear these hats in six different ways." When asked how he figured this out, the teacher showed a chart that presented his thinking is a very organized fashion:

1 = bathing	1	2	3
2 = fire	2	3	2
3 = sailing	3	1	1

The audience uttered a gasp of appreciation when Burns displayed an overhead transparency showing the mathematical thinking of a team of first graders who employed exactly the same methodology. A third grader had a similar scheme and she explained her reasoning in writing: "I don't think there are more than six because every time I tried, I already had done it." Burns stresses the importance of communication in mathematics. "I don't initially put the focus on whether children are right or wrong. I ask them to convince others that their answer is right."

Other teachers in the audience offered different methods for getting the answer, and for each teacher strategy Burns produced similar work done by primary students. Thus the audience saw for themselves—through their own problem solving and the examples of student work—the power of a mathematics problem that can accommodate many levels of mathematical sophistication and methodology. The audience experienced firsthand what Eleanor Duckworth calls "the having of wonderful ideas," the joy of figuring something out yourself—without the barriers of what Burns calls "algorithmic entrenchment." The audience understood through this example that although many math problems may have just one solution, there are a variety of ways to reach that solution. Finally, Burns left the audience thinking about the possibilities inherent in mathematical adventure when she said, "Think about what happens if you have a four-hat day. . . . "

Made Wild by Pompous Catalog

Such an adventure allows children many ways of approach. It allows the least able child to deal with some aspect of the problem while challenging the more able to dig deeper. Eleanor Duckworth says this offers a classroom of children, who are bound to possess a variety of intellectual structures, situations in which they "can come to know parts of the world in new ways." And, as Burns indicates with her suggestion that people think about the four-hat day, a good mathematics lesson is never finished; it offers lots of possibilities.

But teachers always face the demand for certainty, not the elusive promise of possibility. Henry Ward Beecher offered advice to nineteenth-century gardeners that people concerned about children's education would do well to follow. He advised gardeners that they not "be made wild by pompous catalog." It's hard advice to follow, no less in classrooms than in gardens. Certainly curriculum catalogs can be as pompous in their presumptions and promises as any seed catalog: twenty-eight activity cards are billed as "a comprehensive teaching kit"; another set of twelve cards claims to be "everything a teacher needs." Everything for everybody. No claim is too grandiose.

This is not to say that all publishers are the same. Publishers stake out different territories, and the savvy teacher needs to read between the lines to figure out just what that territory is. "Experience the new standard in math instruction," invites one publisher, playing off the NCTM *Standards*. All these buzzwords are used in a single paragraph: estimate, encourage, challenge, exploring, discovering, linking, and applying. Another publisher promises "Step-by-step directions on the Pupil's Edition page" to make "management of manipulative lessons trouble-free."

The difference in appeal is striking: one publisher offers challenge and exploration, the other trouble-free management. One publisher appeals to a more generalized structural tidiness, highlighting their "Planning Chart" at the beginning of each chapter, a chart that "itemizes the objectives of the chapter lessons . . . and shows you exactly how and where the text meets the NCTM *Standards*," thus transmogrifying the *Standards* into nothing more than a skills chart.

We can tell ourselves that teachers take all the posturing and promotional promises in stride; after all, hype surrounds every facet of our lives. We are accustomed to seeing ads for the kitchen implement that slices tomatoes, dices onions, kneads bread dough, grinds coffee beans, polishes the car, eases arthritis pains, and reduces wrinkles—all for the incredible, unbelievable one-time price of $19.95. But long experience in faculty rooms and with focus groups tells me that publishers' hype informs teachers' lives. Catalogs and brochures and advertisements are often their only contact with new products and even new theories; most teachers encounter the NCTM only in catalog references. Of approximately one and a half million K–8 teachers in this country, thirty-six thousand subscribe to the official NCTM publication, *Arithmetic Teacher*, and a large percentage of this figure represents seventh and eighth grade teachers, so the percentage of primary grade teachers who have any direct contact with the NCTM is low.

Teachers get important messages from the catalogs they read; it is a message of pedagogical possibility. You can't read half a dozen catalogs without realizing that these catalogs bring disparate, contradictory visions of what a classroom should be. Like the winter gardener, the summer teacher immersed in catalogs begins to construct her ideal classroom. And most teachers hedge their bets. Few teach only the facts; fewer still devote 100 percent of classroom time to students' constructing their own knowledge. Few teachers choose to plant only one kind of flower; few risk committing themselves to a distinct, exclusionary philosophy. Few teachers maintain a pure worldview of what a classroom should be; most put each finger and toe in as many pedagogical universes as they can stretch to. And so tubs of pattern blocks sit side by side with skill-drill workbooks. To straddle the pedagogical fence—to drill students on math facts and at the same time expect them to think and discover and create for themselves—may be to plant parsnips and orchids side by side. But perhaps a good definition of what it means to be a teacher is to hold two—or maybe even fourteen—contrary notions in one's belief system at the same time.

Some publishers stake out very specific territory. They make no bones about that territory; they do not attempt to disguise skill drill with some high-fallutin' language from the *Standards*, no siree, Mabel. No matter what the pronouncements of professional organizations or blue-ribbon commissions, their market is the teacher who sees pronouncements from the experts come and go while her job remains constant: she is the dispenser of skills and her classroom is a place where children practice their facts. One such catalog is unique among 1991 catalogs in tHat it omits any mention of the NCTM *Standards*. A typical page in the catalog uses the word drill eight times, skills six times, and practice twice. This exercise, called "Math Superstars," is typical of the contents:

A. $13 - 9 = $ ____ $15 - 8 = $ ____ $18 - 9 = $ ____

B. $14 - 7 = $ ____ $15 - 6 = $ ____ $13 - 7 = $ ____

And so on. Catalog blurbs point to other drill pages that can double as timed tests, and pages of drill that "follow the scope and sequence of many current textbooks." The skill-based catalog is heavily sprinkled with such words as *reinforce, master, cover,* and *group drill.*

In sharp contrast, the *Dale Seymour Publications 1991 Catalog K–8 Educational Materials* uses such words as *challenge, develop, stimulate, explore, extend, investigate,* and *build.* Offering innovation and concept development rather than drill or skill practice, the Seymour catalog contains product blurbs promising to "integrate concepts, guide discovery and explorations."

The skill-drill catalog offers "Math Word Problems": "Six to seven problems on each page provide plenty of practice." Here's a sample problem for second graders:

1. Bill has 62 cents in his piggy bank. He spent 38 cents. How much did he have left?

2. John saved 81 cents. He gave 35 cents to his sister. How much does he have now?

Here are third grade problems:

1. John saved $5.95. If he buys a Rainbow game for $3.80, how much will he have left?

2. Tammy wanted to buy the walkie-talkie for $6.86. Her dad gave her $8.81. How much will be left over?

The cover of the *Dale Seymour Catalog* features an opposing classroom view and illustrates one of the many new directions into which mathematics problem solving is moving: a tessellating design drawn by a student. Throughout the catalog nine outstanding tessellating designs, drawn by winners in a contest sponsored by Seymour Publications, are featured. One by Indianapolis first grader Audrea Ramirez is shown on p. 96.

The dichotomy is clear. The *Dale Seymour Catalog* highlights innovative visual thinking and schema transformation; the skill-drill catalog offers "visuals" in the form of simplistic cartoons—a reward for students to color when they finish the skill-drill. These cartoons are billed as "artwork to guarantee student interest," to "motivate students as they add and subtract," and to "cheer students on as they practice multiplication." Yes, a teacher chooses her catalogs, and in so doing, she reveals her pedagogy.

One point to consider about the differing views offered by catalogs and the products they sell is that skill-drill materials are usually authorless. In contrast, materials in such catalogs as Dale Seymour Publications, Creative Publications, and Cuisenaire Company of America are written by people whose names teachers have come to associate with

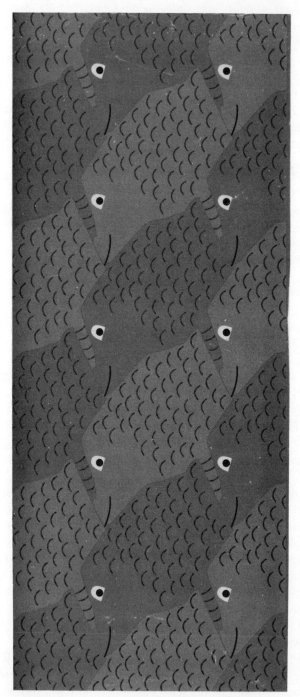

An Indianapolis first grader created The Green Fish, a winning tessellation that appeared in the Dale Seymour Publications catalog.

particular points of view, names such as Marilyn Burns, Patricia Davidson, Kathy Richardson, Mary Baratta-Lorton. When a teacher sees the name, she knows the pedagogy that goes with that name. In contrast, one skill-drill catalog offers "a complete year of sequential math instruction, grade 3" without anywhere in the book giving an author's name. The 96-page book of black-line masters contains lessons "conceived with the purpose of sequentially introducing, carefully teaching, and methodically reinforcing, through drill, the all-important curriculum basics that are definable by rules of facts." But we don't know who conceived it, who did the defining, whose pedagogy this represents, what research base supports it. Critics of skill drill say that what children need is not page after page of drill and practice in column addition, problems that would be better carried out with calculators than with paper and pencil; instead, what children need is to work with one good problem, a problem that can accommodate the very differing abilities and needs of the children in any classroom, a problem that challenges the able learner while at the same time "letting in" the learner who is not yet so able.

"Why Don't Teachers Just Teach and Students Just Learn?"

The content of the ideal mathematics classroom is not an issue that concerns only catalog writers and classroom teachers. Just as you don't have to be a professional gardener to have strong opinions about everything from roses to rutabaga, so, too, does everybody have strong feelings about this thing we call mathematics. It is a topic of increasing concern on the national agenda. Everyone from corporation presidents to congressmen to television anchors to Aunt Mabel has an opinion. Most of them don't hesitate to issue pronouncements: after all, we've all been to school, we've all learned arithmetic. Most of us don't see any mystery in the times tables. "Why don't teachers just teach and students just learn?" is an often-heard complaint. E. D. Hirsch obviously takes this stand in *What Your First Grader Needs to Know;* in something he calls *The Core Knowledge Series,* Hirsch takes his controversial notion of cultural literacy and turns it into a grade-by-grade curriculum.

The NCTM *Standards* insist that school mathematics must move beyond curriculum checklists; the *Standards* are developed to produce change, to prepare our students to live in the twenty-first century. Citing the way new technology has "changed the very nature of the problems important to mathematics and the methods mathematicians use to investigate them," the NCTM advocates that "appropriate calculators should be available to all students at all times." Hirsch's total mention of calculators in the Grade 1 text explains that "People often use a calculator to do arithmetic—after they have learned their addition and subtraction facts by heart! A calculator can add and subtract numbers; it can also do many other things with numbers." Calculators are not mentioned in Hirsch's Grade 2 text.

A Choice of Methods

Skills are the surface issue in this battle. The real issue is not so clearcut. The real issue is what is best for children. Is it better that they memorize a finite set of operations and look good on paper, or is it better that they take the more circuitous route of discovery and understanding? Probably not one teacher in a hundred has resolved this issue to her own satisfaction. Most teachers "accommodate" for each time and place; few resolve the dichotomy once and for all. Most teachers are torn between implementing a constructivist belief system that insists they *cannot* pour, drill, or lecture skills into a child and responding to their own fears and the fears of their administrators, board of education, and community that if they do not continue to pour and drill and lecture math facts, their students will not fare well on standardized tests.

Even Marilyn Burns tells a revealing story about herself to show that she too struggles with this dichotomy, that she too experiences dark moments of doubt. While teaching her multiplication replacement unit to her third graders in California, Burns was in constant communication with third grade teachers in Tucson who were working on the same unit. At one point Burns suggested that Tucson teachers could assign multiplication times tables as homework practice. The 24 Tucson teachers called a meeting, talked over the dilemma, and then faxed letters of protest to Burns, indicating that such a homework practice would violate their belief system, the very belief system Burns had helped them develop in intensive training over several summers. Burns tells the story as an example both of teacher vulnerability to community skill-drill pressures and of teacher willingness to stand up for a principle. She speaks with great pride of the teachers in Tucson who had enough courage of conviction to call their mentor to task.

This is not to suggest that Burns and others advocating a child-centered approach to mathematics don't believe in skills, that they ignore algorithmic proficiency. Nothing could be further from the truth. What they do advocate is that such proficiency should, in the words of the *Standards*, "grow out of the problem situations that have given rise to the need for such algorithms." Furthermore, states the *Standards*, when one needs to calculate to find an answer to a problem, "one should be aware of the choices of methods."

Barbara Denu, first grade teacher at the Goodwood Elementary School in East Baton Rouge, Louisiana, tells a story about such student awareness of problem-solving methods. Denu describes what happened when her students took the California Achievement Test. "The first part of the test involved computation of various types of problems. After seeing what the first part was like, Brandon decided to bring his pocket calculator to school for the second day of testing. After I read the number story twice, Brandon silently took out his calculator and started to work the problem." Having been encouraged all year to figure out the best methods and materials for solving problems, Brandon took a common-sense approach to the achievement test. He did not know that standardized tests operate in a universe all their own, a universe not amenable to common sense. Even though Brandon had made a good assessment of appropriate technology to solve computation problems, his teacher had to take that technology away because standardized test formulators still insist on pencil-and-paper computation.

The NCTM decries classrooms where students passively absorb information, storing it in easily retrievable fragments as a result of repeated practice and reinforcement; the NCTM points to research findings showing that learning does not occur by passive absorption. In sharp contrast, Hirsch offers a curriculum of discrete skills, a pedagogical prescription left over from the behaviorism of the 1970s. Hirsch insists, "The three cardinal principles of early mathematics education are 1) practice, 2) practice, and 3) practice." Although the slogan that "practice makes perfect" has its appeal, any primary grade teacher can produce plenty of horror stories documenting the ineffectiveness and real harm of inappropriate practice. I recall the September morning in the faculty room in my school, where the fourth grade teacher complained bitterly that her incoming students "hadn't been taught their basic facts." Indeed! Those students may not have retained their facts, but the facts had been taught—over and over. And those facts had been memorized, too—over and over. I know because I was their teacher in third grade.

Is the problem simply that I'm a lousy teacher? I don't think so. In every elementary grade, teachers complain that the students haven't learned their "facts." Every year, teachers try to drill those facts into their students again. And the next year's teacher will have the same complaint, anyway. An incredible amount of mathematics instruction time is spent on learning arithmetic facts. Many children are never allowed to do anything else in math class until they have performed satisfactorily on timed tests in math facts. Disembodied facts connected to nothing in children's lives. We torture ourselves and our students with the teaching of too many "facts" too soon. When the time is ripe, when the student is developmentally "ready," we will discover either that he has taught himself the facts, or that the facts are so patently clear to him when the teacher draws his attention to them that his learning will be quick and it will stick instead of being "learned" today and forgotten tomorrow. Inappropriate practice and memorization produces muddled thinking, and, worse, in the end scares the third grade memorizing whiz away from math when he hits seventh grade and discovers he has mastered the surface detail but can't make sense of the underlying structure. Interestingly, on standardized tests, my third graders scored considerably above grade level in problem-solving and at or below grade level in basic computation. Not only could these third graders figure things out, they enjoyed figuring things out. It is not necessary for a nine-year-old to have memorized 9×6 to be able to think mathematically, to engage in "the having of wonderful ideas."

At the end of the year, I asked my students to tell me the best thing about third grade math, and they chose two things: the first was *Anno's Mysterious Multiplying Jar* (Masaichiro and Mitumasa Anno, New York, Philomel, 1983), in which Anno introduces the picture book audience to *factorials* (written as *!*), giving a breathtaking view of a complex mathematical concept. When I read that book to those third graders, they burst into applause when I revealed that 10 factorial is 10!. Anybody who knows third graders knows how much they love exclamation points, and never has ! been so appropriate. Such special topics call on different skills and interests than do arithmetic facts. Special topics don't penalize children who haven't memorized their times tables but provide different avenues to explore, different opportunities to excel. Primary graders can work out 10! on their calculators, and they are impressed to discover that at the end of the story there are 3,628,888 jars. Anno provides that number in notes in the back, but it's a whole lot more exciting for children to discover it for themselves.

Hirsch insists that people experience math anxiety because they are not familiar with the basic arithmetic operations. In his words, "Being instantaneously familiar with the sums and differences of any two digits is even more basic than knowing the alphabet." Whereas Hirsch insists that "practice is the watchword of math," adherents of the NCTM *Standards* posit "recognition and understanding of pattern" as the core of mathematical reasoning. Math anxiety, they say, comes not from lack of familiarity with the basic operations but from lack of recognition of the patterns, the mathematical structure underlying these operations.

Hirsch introduces first grade students to addition, subtraction, place value, geometry, fractions, word problems, and money. The NCTM recommends problem solving (which is a whole different kettle of fish from word problems), communication, reasoning, connections, estimation, number sense, measurement, statistics and probability, fractions, patterns and relationships as well.

Measuring Dinosaurs, the Mayflower, and Pigs

Measurement is a good case in point. Here is Hirsch's advice to second graders on the topic of measurement: "Learn to measure the length of different objects using a ruler marked in inches." Hirsch concedes that children can also use a tape measure. Classrooms built around a process-oriented mathematics do a lot with measurement. Starting in kindergarten, children measure with their bodies and their books, with rods, cubes, gummy bears, and toothpicks. Children learn they can measure with just about anything that isn't nailed down. Children measure, not just to find the precise length of a particular object but to discover relationships.

Mary Bacon's kindergartners at Goodwood Elementary School combine exploration of number sense with rough measurement by exploring how many children it takes to equal the length of some dinosaurs they've been reading about:

brontosaurus:	88 feet
	25 children
tyrannosaurus rex:	50 feet long
	14 children
triceratops:	30 feet
	$8\frac{1}{2}$ children
stegosaurus:	20 feet
	6 children

Note that they learn in the process that things don't always measure in even units, and hence the need for $8\frac{1}{2}$ children.

Nicholas

Head 22 inches

smile 4 inches

arm 22 inches

shoe 9 inches

Primary graders in East Baton Rouge, Louisiana, draw numerical self-portraits (*shown above and on pp. 103–105*).

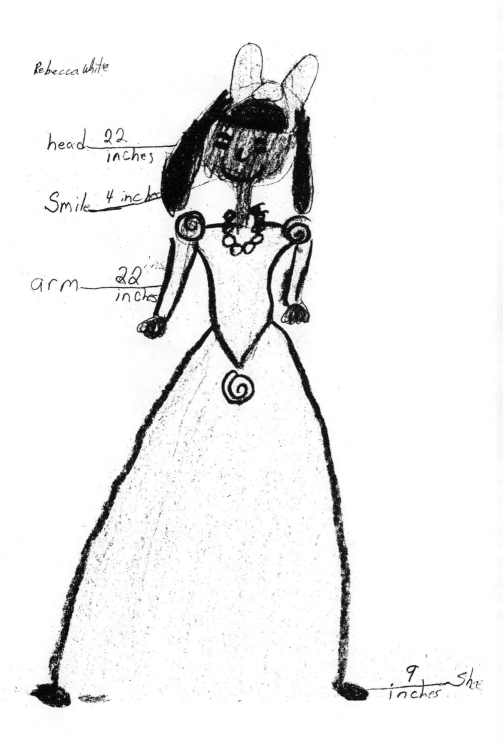

Rebecca White

head — 22 inches

Smile — 4 inches

arm — 22 inches

9 inches She

Camille Broadhurst

head 20 inches

smile 3 inches

arm 22 inches

shoe 10 inches

At the Allen Field School in Milwaukee, Wisconsin, Marlene Gowecki's first graders measure off the 90-by-25-foot dimensions of the Mayflower on the playground, and then use their own bodies to construct a human model of the Mayflower. Then children from other classes, representing the 106 Pilgrims and 24 sailors aboard the original vessel, get "into" the Mayflower. In addition to adding to their experience of number sense, everyone gets a "feel" of what it is like to crowd 130 people into an area that size. Children take the experience of this real-life mathematical model back into their classroom as they study the Pilgrims' voyage to North America.

When I invited first through sixth grade teachers to use the book *Farmer Mack Measures His Pig* by Tony Johnson (New York, Harper and Row, 1986) as a springboard for student investigation and invention in mathematics, students proved themselves very much equal to the task. First, teachers asked their students, "How would you measure a pig?" By leaving the task open-ended, teachers encourage students to think for themselves rather than rely on a recipe provided by a text or a teacher. The variety of approaches students bring to such a project gives their teachers important information for planning future work. Students reveal themselves as inventors, psychologists, and dreamers. Some children at every grade level suggest sneaking up on the pig and measuring it while it is asleep. Others suggest killing the pig first. A fourth grader writes, "I'd tell that pig if he didn't slow down, I'd make bacon out of him."

Fourth grade seems to be the time when children start inventing complicated contraptions to achieve their goals. One student suggests, "Put him in a box with the middle cut out. Then his middle would be sticking out so I could measure it." Here's another invention: "Invent a foot-tying machine that measures while it's tying and then releases the pig as soon as the measuring is done." Another student offers, "Shove one end of a tape measure into the pig's food and when the pig eats the food you hold on to the other end and hold it to his tail."

Student psychologists suggest:

- I'd measure while I pet him.
- Offer him corn flakes.
- Let him sleep in my bed.
- Make him a mud bath, and while he's enjoying it, I'd measure him.
- I would ignore him until he started following me around. Then I'd feed him and pat him on the head while I measured him.

- I'd calm him down first and let him know I wasn't going to hurt him.

One fourth grader has a suggestion no one else thought of: "I'd ask his permission." And a sixth grader shows the humorous practicality made famous in a classic Scottish recipe for haggis. If you want to measure a pig, the student writes, "First, catch the pig." Sixth graders also show themselves to be different from younger students in other ways. "Get a girl pig for the boy pig. While they are talking, you can measure them."

Once children have thought about measuring a pig, they are ready to move on to other things. When asked, "Is there something else that would be difficult to measure?" some children give answers that are common to all grades: kangaroo, skyscraper, butterfly, volcano. Many children name the biggest thing they can think of: the Appalachian mountain range, the World Trade Center, Halley's comet, the whole universe. A few realize that small things might also be difficult to measure: the width of a blade of grass or a strand of hair or a spider's eggs. One student says it would be hard to measure the width of your memory span.

When asked, "Is there anything you'd like to measure, some thing you've wondered about?" children in grades one through three mention things like their dog or the Mississippi River. The fourth graders' lists are longer, reflecting an expanding fund of topics they wonder about: blue whales, Bigfoot, the Amazon River, Leaning Tower of Pisa, black holes. By the sixth grade, this curiosity seems to have dried up for many children. Nearly half of the sixth graders can't think of anything they'd like to measure and are surprised that anybody would ask such a question. Sixth graders know the way things are "s'pozed to be" in math class—they're supposed to answer questions, not ask them. Those children who do respond come up with provocative possibilities: "I wonder what is the distance to heaven; I would like to know how long the world would be if it were flattened out."

Although it is disheartening to realize that traditional skill-drill schoolwork has smothered the spark of curiosity in many children by the time they're eleven years old, there is still room for optimism in the responses of a few of their peers. These children show interests touching on the great ideas that have ever concerned man the questioner: topics in astronomy, cartography, meteorology, architecture, psychology, and metaphysics.

In his preface to Stephen Hawking's *A Brief History of Time* (London, Bantam Press, 1988), Carl Sagan says he has met children "who want to know what a black hole looks like; what is the smallest piece of matter; why we remember the past and not the future; how it is, if there was chaos early, that there is apparently order today; and why there IS a universe." A Hirschian curriculum does not consider the child as thinker and questioner but positions the child as receiver of discrete skills. For Hirsch, knowledge is "out there," something to be delivered to the student according to a specific chronology rather than personally and socially constructed by the student.

The measure-a-pig project builds on the idea that when children measure a lot of things they are both gaining number sense and practical practice in the computation skills they're learning. Measuring activities also provide opportunities for interdisciplinary learning. Taking 100 inches around Farmer Mack's pig as a starting point, teachers invite their students to do two things: "Estimate 100 inches, and then find 100 inches in your environment."

You can learn a lot about a child by noting where and how he "looks" for his answers. One boy looks around his classroom and guesses: "the bulletin board, the chalkboard, the table, five big windows." That last answer takes him outside and his list continues: "the big tree outside, the telephone lines." Then he starts dreaming, "a big pony, a giant's silverware . . . "

Some third graders announce that they must be 100 inches long and are astounded at what a tape measure reveals—that they range from 51 to 57 inches in length. Three boys are curious to know how many books it would take to reach 100 inches, and soon their classmates see 136 books trail down the hallway. Another group discovers that just about anything can be a fraction of 100, so they begin measuring each other and parts of themselves. The number of big toes it takes to make 100 inches provides an outlet for fourth-grade humor. Who said mathematics has to be somber all the time?

Reflecting on Problem Solving (or Learning from Experience)

An important component in all of this measurement, as in all mathematical investigation, is student reflection. Students are asked to describe and evaluate their methods for estimating 100 inches. Here is what they write:

> This activity was harder than I expected because it was hard to picture the object I was trying to estimate. I tried to figure out how

many rulers across it was. If it was about eight-and-a-half rulers across, then I knew it would be about 100 inches. I think my method was effective in some ways because I estimated a few things correctly. But it wasn't always effective, especially when I measured perimeter. I sort of forgot what perimeter was and I was thinking of height, so the perimeter of something usually turned out to be longer than I expected.

—Robyn

Of the four people at my table, one of us (Kevin) happened to be exactly 5 feet tall. He'd stand or lie next to the object. We'd estimate that there were about 3 feet above him. Then we hoped we'd end up with 8 feet or 96 inches. About 40 percent of the time, using Kevin worked. Two times we got 96 inches, one time we got 97 inches, and another time we got 102 inches.

—Jane

I thought of a very tall person lying down on the thing I was going to measure. My method of estimating didn't work too well because I didn't get very close to 100 inches on anything.

—Joe

I thought this was pretty easy. All you have to do is picture in your mind a person who's about 8 feet tall.

—Matt

The method I used was to think of how many feet 100 inches made. Then I thought of some basketball players and added a foot to them. My method was more effective using length than perimeter because I couldn't imagine something straightened out. But for length, my method worked.

—Alison

I pictured a tape measure because it has more room than a ruler. I have no idea why some of our guesses weren't effective. I guess they were just pretty lousy guesses.

—Beth

It didn't work very well to use a person for estimating because the person wasn't exactly 100 inches. She was 54 inches.

—Judy

Most sixth graders aren't accurate most of the time in their estimates of 100 inches, but they reach the conclusion that their experiment is a success anyway. They realize that even though they might not have found 100 inches, they have discovered something important; they've found out something about length, and some of them have gained insight into their own problem-solving strategies, known in the jargon of our trade as *metacognition*. This attitude of not depending on a single right answer as the sole criterion of the success of an investigation fits right in with scientific research and discovery, where negative results can be more important than positive ones. If a child—or a scientist—can recognize that three wrong answers are the result of bad methodology, a blind alley, or whatever, then he's much better off than if he had produced one lucky right answer. J. B. S. Haldane, a noted British scientist, observes, "Amateur scientists commonly fail because they set out to prove something rather than to arrive at the truth, whatever that may be." Teachers who assign a task like this 100-inches-estimation project want their students to move one step further in number sense by finding out how to find out things—not merely to turn in a tedious worksheet filled with all the 100-inch objects in the school. Finding 100 inches can be a trivial exercise or a gateway to discovery. It all depends on the teacher. And the child.

Writing in *The New Yorker* more than a decade ago, Alfred Adler complains that textbooks don't communicate what mathematics is really about, where it is going. "What really matters is the communication of the spirit of mathematics. It is a spirit that is active rather than contemplative—a spirit of disciplined search for adventures of the intellect. Only an adventurer can really tell of adventures."

Manipulatives: Pattern Blocks and Pedagogy

Ask in what one way all the K–3 Math Projects resemble each other and the answer has to be *manipulatives,* those brightly colored geometric pattern blocks, interlocking Unifix cubes, ancient Chinese tangram puzzles, two-color counters, geoboards, and Cuisenaire rods that fill primary grade classroom shelves from Conecuh County, Alabama, to Albuquerque, New Mexico. Patricia Cassady, a K–3 project director in Conecuh County, leads a project that has put a collection of manipulatives into every K–2 classroom in the county. A visitor to the schools sees immediately the significance of the decision, the value placed on manipulatives. These classrooms are not rich in supplies. Even the kindergartens, typically crowded with a richness of colorful objects elsewhere in the country, are pretty much bare-bones in this county. Geographically situated in a rural area midway between Mobile and Montgomery, Conecuh County is among the most sparsely populated and economically depressed regions in the state. If classrooms are bare, so are teachers' wallets. Cassady's uniqueness in professional organization membership is not surprising in a state where the top salary available for a teacher with a master's degree is $27,000. It doesn't matter how long she has taught, how many courses she has taken to increase her knowledge, that is the most she can make.

Nonetheless, when Miriam Callison, supervisor of curriculum and instruction in nearby Butler County, announced a four-day summer

Cuisenaire rods are a collection of rectangular rods of ten lengths and ten colors. Here a child uses rods to explore different combinations that add up to ten.

teacher workshop (with no stipends available to teachers) on the use of manipulatives, 90 percent of the faculty attended. Although the target audience was K–2 teachers, some third grade teachers sought—and received—permission to attend. In my travels I have seen this phenomenon over and over: when teachers see a good thing, when they see a way to revitalize their craft, they want in. You can never overestimate the desire of teachers to find a better way.

Middle-Aged Tricks and Triumphs

It seems somewhat ironic that manipulatives are suddenly the hot new thing in education. Manipulatives have been available on the education market for thirty years or more. Unifix cubes, for example, were first introduced in 1953. And despite plenty of research documenting the value of providing a concrete way to help students understand mathematical concepts, manipulatives have never really caught on. Thomas Kuhn suggests that a paradigm shift takes twenty-five years to install itself; it has been suggested, not entirely in jest, that you must wait for everybody clutching the old paradigm to die off. I suspect that may be true in pre-service education. For widespread change to take place in colleges of education, we are in desperate need of some new paradigm-holders. It's hard to teach old dogs new tricks. Old teachers are another matter. In schools across the country, I see middle aged teachers learning lots of new tricks. I see twenty-five-year-veteran teachers grabbing on to new ideas—and changing their basic beliefs about how children learn best. I find this nothing short of incredible. Teachers who are well respected for their classroom expertise are abandoning their tried-and-true methods and learning something new.

O.K., not everybody. Although about 80 percent of the teachers whose classrooms I visited are obviously intrigued by manipulatives, although these teachers talk of using their workbook monies to purchase manipulatives, they still fill their bulletin boards with skill-drill worksheets. The hard step is not getting manipulatives into classrooms; the hard step is replacing the workbook mindset with a new paradigm. One teacher's journal is revealing. She uses manipulatives, not as an end in themselves but as a means to an end—and a short term end at that. She sets up each manipulative in a different math center in her classroom and reports: "The children really enjoy the different manipulatives, and they are a good management enforcer. Bad behavior stops immediately when I mention withdrawing center privileges." Bribery and threats work in the short term. So do cattle prods.

On the other hand, Sandra Young, second grade teacher and math specialist at Dr. Phillips Elementary School in Orlando, Florida, is typical of teachers who beat themselves up for not knowing everything there is to know about a given manipulative—yesterday. She writes in her journal, "Yesterday, attending the fractions workshop, I felt guilty about not knowing some of the manipulatives. I realize how lacking I am in this area." The math journal, which most of the math specialists groused about in the beginning and continued to grumble over all year—teachers are busy and not used to such regular reflection—proves invaluable in promoting and supporting teacher change in ways that are only tiny in their surface appearance. Young is lucky in that her district supports its push to integrate manipulatives into the program with weekly visits of district math resource people to each math specialist's classroom. Muffet Fox, district math resource person, reads Young's journal and reminds Young she has been a math specialist for only a few days and that she has plenty of time to learn about those fraction pieces. It is unlikely that Young would have voiced her feelings of inadequacy in a face-to-face conversation; and if Fox hadn't seen the self-doubt in the journal, she wouldn't have been able to allay the fears. Throughout the year, Fox's journal responses tell each teacher she isn't alone in her fears, that other teachers throughout the district are experiencing similar trauma.

But Fox doesn't just reassure. In another classroom, when Fox sees that first graders are being asked to do column addition for a graph, she asks them if they have a calculator. "What's that?" asks a student. Fox quickly locates one and shows the student how it will help her. Later, Fox casually works mention of calculators into a conversation with the teacher. She doesn't say, "You should have made calculators available during this lesson," but asks where the teacher stores them, suggesting they need to be accessible to the students at all times, not just for structured lessons. In the course of the conversation the teacher admits she's been nervous about how to use the calculators, so Fox volunteers to "come back next week and teach with you." Orlando project director Linda Levine says, "You can effect change in a large and diverse district like ours if you are constantly there—supporting and nudging." Levine adds, "But this kind of supervision isn't cheap."

Albuquerque uses a different model for supporting teachers' attempts to change their belief systems. Project director Lois Folsom visits classrooms regularly, jumping in to help with whatever is going on when she appears, as well as teach demonstration lessons, but Folsom believes the real strength of their model is having two math specialists in a building to support each other. "Two people together spread the word much more quickly and effectively than two people separately," insists Folsom.

Reading the Labels

Some districts seem to offer no support. The manipulatives arrive, and the specialist tries to figure out how to use them. One specialist uses her lunch break to teach demonstration lessons on new materials that she hasn't used herself. She reads the manufacturer's blurbs and hopes for the best. Another teacher holds open house for her colleagues before school and at lunch, inviting them to come in and browse. The lack of genuine training for the specialists seems abusive, but one specialist points out that a real camaraderie has developed out of the lunchtime meetings. "They know I'm not really an expert, and we're exploring together." The specialist adds that in six months she's had lunch with more colleagues more often than in her previous twelve years of teaching. The project director says part of the problem is that teachers won't wait. As soon as the manipulatives arrive, they want to use them.

Pat Hess, the liaison between the Exxon Education Foundation, the NCTM, and the project sites, is adamant that if a district is committed to changing the way mathematics is taught, then every classroom must have its own core supply of manipulatives. And, says Hess, if there is a larger, shared community supply, then it must be visible: "Put it alongside the copy machine," she advises project heads. Hess warns project heads that if they rely only on a community supply of manipulatives and do not put buckets of pattern blocks, cubes, and so forth in every class-room, then it is likely that the use of manipulatives will be, at best, sporadic and unfocused; at worst, they won't be used at all. Hess's advice proves to be prophetic. Teachers in one school voted to put all the manipulatives in a central location rather than in individual class-rooms, and now the math specialist is the only teacher in the building using them. Hess gets a gleam in her eye as she talks about this. She will move in on that situation and change it. An element unique to the K–3 Math Project is that the Foundation's interest in sites has not ended with the disbursement of monies. Hess visits sites again and again, to cheer them on and to get those manipulatives into children's hands.

Some schools use the math specialist in a role similar to the old-style remedial teacher. This person visits each classroom once a week and teaches a manipulative-based lesson unrelated to anything else that is going on in the classroom. In an open-pod school where teachers and administrators are (rightly) very concerned about the noise level, each class travels to the math specialist's room in a separate building, the only classroom with walls and a door, once a week for their manipulative lesson. The weaknesses in such an approach are obvious. Although the specialist has the opportunity to hone a few showcase lessons, these lessons stand alone, separate from what the children's "real" teacher does the rest of the week. And young children are very quick to pick up on which math "counts" and which is peripheral. The specialist has no opportunity to observe children through the day, to spot that moment when a particular manipulative would be perfect for a particular child. Even when the classroom teacher stays in the room when the specialist does her dog-and-pony show, she isn't necessarily paying any attention. In one room, the classroom teacher corrects skill-drill papers while the math specialist offers a whole-group lesson on tangrams.

The tangram lesson itself is lockstep. Time is limited. The specialist has only 40 minutes, and the students aren't "hers"; once she finishes this lesson, she must rush off to repeat it with another group. She jumps right into the lesson: "Boys and girls, turn to page 11." There is no free play. Every child is on page 11—until they are told, "Slide your pieces off, and look at page 12."

The specialist does not know the children's names. It's not clear why, but she hasn't been in this classroom in over a month. The pace is much too slow for some children. They try to sneak a few pages ahead but get caught and reprimanded. "It's vital you stay with the group. If you try to skip ahead, you will miss something important, and then you won't know what to do." I feel these third graders' affront when she says, "When I did this with first graders . . ."

Other children are expected to sit and wait while one child tries to recreate a figure on the overhead projector. The class begins to squirm; I want to squirm too. I didn't know that tangrams could be so boring—or that 40 minutes could be so interminable. When the squirming and poking gets a bit more palpable, the specialist reminds the children, "Who remembers what our rule is for the end of the math lesson—if we cooperate?" A child volunteers, "We get to mess around with our shapes."

The teacher corrects him. "We get to experiment; the word is experiment. With TANGRAMS." She exaggerates the pronunciation. "What are these called, class? . . . That's right, TANGRAMS." Whatever the word is, when the basic premises of manipulatives are violated in the name of behavior control and standardization, I say, "Stick it in your ear." The students would be better off attending to the workbook drill pages. At least there they get to work at their own pace.

Eight Bears at a Picnic and Classroom Pandemonium

In contrast to the tight control evident in the tangram lesson, another math specialist 1200 miles away works in her own classroom filled with a bountiful supply of manipulative materials. I don't know that I have ever seen so many manipulatives in one classroom. Since it is toward the end of the school year, one can assume she has intimate knowledge of these first graders. Nonetheless, the classroom is seemingly without structure or accountability of any kind. A large, bright and cheerful place, children are wandering around with no apparent destination. I start wandering too, feeling more like I'm in Grand Central Station than a schoolroom. Finally the teacher says, "I'll turn off the fan so it won't be so noisy in here." Who could tell the fan was on? The fan was definitely not the problem. With the fan off, she calls the children to their chairs so she can teach a whole-group lesson on problem solving. Children have piles of brightly colored Teddy Bear Counters on their desks (now that suppliers have caught on to the popularity of colored objects for children to sort and count, the market is flooded with teddy bears, dinosaurs, race cars, and so on), and the teacher announces they are going to write their own teddy bear math problems on the overhead screen. The teacher models a problem. Then Jerry walks to the overhead projector and writes his problem: "8 bears went to a picnic and 8 bears left. That's it." Jerry sits down. Hardly anybody is paying any attention, and Jerry remains deadpan, but I wonder if he isn't rehearsing for a spot on the David Letterman show. I'm wondering if all of us couldn't be on Letterman. Not only are the children not paying any attention to Jerry's problem, they are throwing the Teddy Bear Counters they are supposed to be using to solve Jerry's problem at each other. (The plan is that you would push eight counters to a central spot on your desk and then take away or add however many the problem dictated—in this case, eight would be removed—and see what you have left.) And I'm sitting here in the middle of this chaos taking notes. Yes, I am writing all this down. Like Jerry, I remain deadpan; the faster I write, the faster the teddy bears fly. The teacher's cheerful enthusiasm becomes frenetic. I wonder if it is desperation masquerading as elation. I wonder if it's because there are visitors in the room that she pretends not to see the Teddy Bear Counters flying through the air. She continues to call children up to the overhead to write teddy bear problems, but none of the problems is as good as Jerry's. The rest of the problems are on par with the ones that are on the worksheets stacked on the teacher's desk. They are apples and oranges masquerading as teddy bears. Teddy Bear Counters whiz by me as I leave to visit another classroom. I hope the teacher turns the fan back on. She looks flustered.

Engaged in Mathematics

Students in Pam Spencer's second grade classroom at Field School in Columbia, Missouri, use a variety of manipulative materials as they rotate among activity stations:

- Unifix cubes—measurement
- Pattern blocks—multiplication
- Multilink patterns—patterns
- Learninglinks—multiplication
- Fraction pieces
- Topcards—addition
- Bears in Boats—subtraction

Thus, children work on several skills at the same time; they don't have to "master" subtraction facts before they move to fractions or multiplication. Spencer does not tell them that the pattern blocks and Learninglinks activities both deal with multiplication, but Jeanne discovers

Pattern blocks are a collection of six geometric shapes in six colors. Children use them to explore such topics as patterns, symmetry, area, perimeter, fractions, and functions.

this on her own. "Hey! I was multiplying over there, and now I'm doing it here! It's different but it's kind of the same."

Jeanne has made a profound discovery. The same mathematical concept can be approached from different angles by using different manipulatives. Given time themselves to explore the potential of manipulative materials, teachers learn that what really matters is not so much whether they have students work with pattern blocks or geoboards; what really matters is their view of what children can—and should—do with these materials. What really matters is that the teacher have a belief system firmly in place, a belief system that extends far beyond the use of any specific learning tool.

Spencer points to the value of having the supplies readily available. While her class is reading *Sam and Minute the Man*, someone gets the idea of counting all the minutemen in the book. And so they grab their calculators and do it.

Should Students Discover or Memorize?

Sally Walker, first grade teacher in Las Cruces, New Mexico, is as excited as Andrew when he invents a pattern during "free exploration" with his geoboard. This point is significant; free exploration is not a concept that is satisfied during the first fifteen minutes the children are exposed to manipulatives and then never returned to again. Children need to do what "real" mathematicians do—explore and invent for the rest of their lives. And so, late in the school year Walker's students are "still" freely exploring. Andrew brings Walker a pattern: five rubber bands placed horizontally and five rubber bands placed vertically. Andrew says, "I've made four squares and four squares. That makes eight. And there are eight and eight—that makes . . ." He pauses and then continues, "seven and seven are 14, so eight and eight are 16." Andrew is pleased, and so is his teacher. This sixteen-year-veteran teacher says she is reinvigorated by her new training. She says, "I have a doubles chart on the back wall, but isn't it ever so much better that Andrew discovered this on his own?" Walker adds, "I enjoy teaching math more than ever before and I would never go back to teaching math from a traditional textbook. Seeing the children discover their own math makes me proud to be a teacher."

Another significance here is that Walker is not trying to streamline and shortcut the children's messing around with manipulatives; she is not preventing deviant use. Because she does not focus on the concept Andrew should get from geoboards, he makes a profound discovery on his own. My twenty years in my own classroom tells me that children's significant discoveries are never in the lesson plan. Almost no education outsiders, and a minority of insiders, understand this very basic fact about the way schools work.

Certainly, E. D. Hirsch offers a contrasting view of how schools should work. Hirsch would have Andrew memorize that $7 + 7 = 14$. The mathematics program spelled out in Hirsch's curriculum does not mention manipulatives. Hirsch is concerned with arithmetic, which, in his words, has "to do with numbers and counting and adding and subtracting." Period. Later he advises children, "By the end of the first grade, you should know all the addition and subtraction facts up to 12 by heart." Period. Hirsch has a soul brother in that self-assured schoolmaster Thomas Gradgrind in Dickens's *Hard Times*:

Now, what I want is, Facts. Teach these boys and girls nothing but Facts. Facts alone are wanted in Life. Plant nothing else, and root out everything else. You can only form the minds of reasoning animals upon Facts: nothing else will ever be of any service to this. . . Stick to Facts, sir!

Actually, Andrew did learn plenty of facts. The difference is that he did not memorize them; he discovered them.

Significant Choices or Worksheet Workout?

If we do not organize our classrooms so that children acquire the capacity for significant choice, how are they ever going to survive in the real world? If all the choices during the school day are made by the teacher (or, worse, by the supervisor), then the most important thing about education is lost.

Something occurs to me during the tangram lesson and again during a highly routinized whole-class geoboard lesson, one where the teacher has decided ahead of time exactly what the children should learn. One of the basic tenets of the "new" reading is that the children will see the teacher as a genuine model of what she believes in. Hence when students are engaged in sustained silent reading, the teacher is also reading. She is reading adult books; she is not sitting at her desk correcting grammar worksheets. When students are writing, so is the teacher. So I raise a tough question: Must a teacher do "real" mathematics if her students are to believe she values it? How often do children see teachers—or any other adults—engaged in mathematics? How often do they see teachers messing around with tangram pieces, making a tessellating pattern with blocks, making a graph, investigating a problem that connects to their real lives outside the classroom? I'm not talking about demonstration lessons on the overhead; I'm talking about genuine, exploratory doing math, where teachers engage in their own projects for the sheer pleasure—or necessity—of it.

Filling a classroom with brightly colored manipulatives is not synonymous with giving children (or teachers) choices. In fact, in some classrooms manipulatives are used as a form of control and repression. Different manipulatives are put in different areas of the room, called learning stations. The children rotate every 10 or 15 minutes while the teacher takes reading groups or tends to other matters. Each manipulative station has worksheets for the students to fill in, documenting that they haven't been wasting their time—not quite, anyway. But manipulative busywork doesn't look a whole lot different from workbook busywork. There is no discussion, no probing; students do what they are supposed to do—fill in the blanks in someone else's structure. They don't ask questions, don't talk over discoveries; in short, they don't think. They fill in those worksheets quietly so as not to disturb the teacher's reading group instruction.

This just goes to prove that good intentions aren't enough. If school districts do not have a basic faith in teachers and children, then they cheerfully and rigorously take the steps necessary to puritanically design out any deviant possibilities—with manipulatives and everything else. Many districts that advertise themselves as being at the forefront of educational practices operate from elaborate, cross-referenced, computerized master plans constructed to ensure that every child in the district "covers" the same material, as though teachers were in the business of installing carpet or manufacturing soap. These master plans contain what they call mission statements that include the following: "100 percent of the staff will use effective instructional strategies identified by the district."

Loud alarm bells must go off. That isn't merely loony pedagogy; that is a loony prescription for any kind of human behavior except, maybe, installing round pegs into round holes. As any savvy teacher can attest, management sharpshooters with briefcases filled with "effective" strategies come and go. But even more than that, when anybody makes this kind of claim, it's time to count the silverware. Where in this life do we get 100 percent of anything? And why would anybody want 100 percent of something called instructional strategies identified by a district? (Never mind investigating how a district defines "same.") Surely there must be room in every system for at least one oddball who, in response to "effective," echoes Bartleby and says, "I'd rather not."

But it's a whole lot less expensive—and less messy—to buy a management plan than to train teachers. So a curriculum supervisor who bills his district as being on "the cutting edge of education" gets manipulative materials into the classroom in the most efficient and inexpensive manner possible. In lieu of training, teachers received a detailed management guide showing which manipulatives teach which skill and listing the corresponding skill pages in all the textbooks, workbooks, filmstrips, and computer programs in the district, as well as the pages in such supplementary programs as *AIMS*, *Box It or Bag It*, and *Math Their Way*. So if a teacher is teaching, say, single-digit addition, she is informed she can use base ten blocks, counters, Unifix cubes, or calculators. She doesn't have to worry about figuring out anything for herself. If, say, she is teaching measurement, she is informed to:

- Give guided practice using Link-Its to measure various items.

- Once students have achieved mastery, distribute the activity sheet. Students will measure the pictured items and record the results.

How Long is the Principal's Shoe?

I gladly concede that it is helpful for teachers to receive administrative blessings on the use of manipulatives; perhaps in a weak moment I might even concede that the district level imprimatur on a chart delineating all the "skills" specific manipulatives can deliver, cross-checked with all those textbook pages and other resources, could be helpful. So why am I so nervous? The activity sheet, delivered to every teacher (of the appropriate grade level) in the district, tells the tale. In the course of one "lesson" the child is to fill in this worksheet:

My pencil is ——— Link-Its long.

My book is ——— Link-Its long.

My shoe is ——— Link-Its long.

This kind of activity sheet removes all initiative, all choice, all crea-tivity from the child. My reaction may seem cranky, but it is, in fact, not cranky but deep-seated, fundamental rage. All this is too organized and too limiting: too organized for the teacher, too organized for the child. How lovely it is when a teacher just asks, "What could you measure and what will you measure with?" and then, after measuring everything in sight for a few days, three children come up with the offbeat idea of measuring their shoes. And this happens all the time: it is a fact of human nature and curiosity and ingenuity that children will come up with great things to measure. I can bear witness that it happens in class-rooms across the country. Educational systems management organizers do not need to tell children what to measure. And if children don't come up with the shoe idea, has anybody lost out?

What if, instead, children were asked to:

1. Figure out what they were going to measure, and

2. Figure out what their measurement units would be, and

3. Figure out how to record their data, and

4. Figure out the most interesting way to present their findings to their classmates.

This could lead to graphs of the shortest and longest items in the room. Children could explore, as they did in one school, to find out who had the biggest shoe in the school. But the excitement and exhilaration of asking the principal if you can measure his shoe is diluted if it is the teacher's idea and not the child's. The idea is diluted still further when it arrives by administrative fiat, when every child is measuring exactly the same things.

Time for Tomfoolery up against the Skill Treadmill

By linking manipulatives so closely with specific skills, by telling teachers you use Link-Its for this and Unifix cubes for that, district policymakers set the manipulatives up for failure. It is entirely natural that teachers newly introduced to manipulatives see them as bright, exotic playthings—definitely an "extra" to their busy basic program. If management guides reinforce the message that the only reason we have manipulatives is to enhance the teaching of prescribed basic skills, then the teacher who is short of time and/or money will skip over the manipulative activity. And get right to the skills.

This is a very difficult issue, and we are talking about hardworking, well-meaning people struggling with tough questions. For teachers, the tough issue is not technique, learning "how" to use the manipulatives. For many teachers, who have survived rigorous training, including courses in algebra and calculus, the tough issue is still ahead. They must come to grips both with the purpose to which they are putting manipulatives and their basic beliefs about how children learn. A number of teachers speak in high moral terms of getting rid of the workbooks and using the money for manipulatives, but then they use those manipulatives in pretty much the same ways they used the workbooks: busywork to keep children reasonably quiet while the teacher is occupied with small group instruction.

Teachers need to ask themselves for what purpose children are rotating through a host of manipulative stations at 15-minute intervals. What children need is a lot of uninterrupted time to do mathematics, to mess around in the broad, complex, and wonderfully varied territory of number sense. Fifteen minutes simply won't cut it. If children are using manipulatives, they need plenty of time to experiment, to engage in "off-task" speculation and tomfoolery. This is a new idea for most elementary classrooms, where the common practice is for the teacher to list on the board a dozen items children are to get through independently—and quietly. Studies show that a child typically "gets through" over two hundred worksheets a week. One of the weaknesses of setting up a classroom into "centers" for math time is that center activity can become almost as meaningless as workbook pages: the child is still rushing through somewhere between fifty and two hundred worksheets a week. Too often, it rather looks like the people in charge are shoving skill-drill out the door and then sneaking it back in through the window. If teachers and children are to take "centers" seriously, then the children will need some time when the center is their choice, not another stop on the skill rotation treadmill. They will need to be able to stay at that center for an extended time—a few days or a few weeks. The children will need to be able to decide when they've had enough.

Who's in Charge?

The trouble is that in some districts neither teachers nor children are given any room to make decisions. Even though they bill themselves as "shared decision-making schools and site-based managers," in reality they are a mandate-driven, top-down hierarchy, one where an objectives-based testing system drives a skills curriculum. There is in such a system what Rexford Brown calls a "grim sense of mistrust in teachers' abilities to teach and monitor their students' work." I would take Brown one step further and point also to the grim sense of mistrust in children's ability to monitor their work. Brown says that in such a system, "teachers don't have any choice but to position themselves as implementers of programs and procedures." Administrators use a Hunter evaluation model, placing a high premium on direct instruction and positing learning as a sequence of skill mastery. Teachers are required to format instruction in a sequence with its own peculiar terminology: anticipatory set, stating the objective, direct instruction, checking for understanding, guided practice, closure, and independent practice.

Socks and Bottle Caps

A lot of people miss the point. They think the point is getting those wonderful manipulative materials into the classrooms. But the real point is the creative potential of the teachers and children in those classrooms. The hard reality of the schoolroom is that you can't send in a purchase order for the things that really matter. Concrete, hands-on materials are wonderful, but you don't always need a purchase order for them, either. The first week of school, Glenda Stone brings two large sacks full of loose socks into her first grade classroom at the W. O. Palmer Elementary School in Greenville, Alabama. "My husband's socks need to be sorted into pairs," she tells her students. "Can you estimate how many pairs there might be in this pile?" School has only been in session a week, so children have not had much opportunity to hone their number sense, and estimates range from 10 pairs to 1000. All the estimates are put on the board. Children sit in two large circles and, working in pairs, they sort the socks into pairs. One child worries that he doesn't want to touch somebody else's dirty socks. "No, honey, they're clean," Stone assures him. When all the socks are sorted into pairs, Stone asks, "Who can tell me how we can find out how many pairs of socks we have?" There is a lot of talk and then a child observes that each of them has two pairs. After some more discussion, the children decide to count by two's. They figure out that there are 42 pairs. Since one child's estimate up on the board is 43, everyone expresses great amazement at how close he was. Stone points to lots of guesses that are close to show children that a guess doesn't have to be "right" to be good, a principle she will come back to again and again throughout the year.

Stone tells her students, "I've been teaching twenty-five years, and this is the first time I've brought socks to school. I just got up this morning and told my husband, "I need all your socks—and I need them separated." He is used to such requests; last year, when Stone's group counted to 1000 for the first time, her husband, vice president at a local bank, brought in a $1000 bill for them to hold. Stone muses, "Can you imagine? I used to teach math from a book. But then I found out that there is math all around us." She points out that just having manipulative materials available brings change. "You can't do things the same when you have different materials to work with."

Stone confesses, "I was nervous about this kind of math . . . because I didn't understand it. I'm structured. But I'm learning. In a very deep way, this makes sense to me. And I know I can learn more. I know I can reach for another kind of structure."

A parent volunteer who is helping with the sock-sorting agrees that this is a wonderful way for children to learn mathematics. This parent, who works a split shift at the post office, comes to the classroom whenever she's on break from her job—and her children aren't even in this class. She says she likes being a part of a kind of mathematics that makes sense.

Early in my own career I was fortunate enough to be left free of administrative interference to create a classroom that gave children and me time and space to explore. Through benign neglect, I found myself in charge, and because my experience as a teacher showed me that neither child nor teacher should make all the classroom decisions, I invited the children to take charge. In that room children chose their topics and materials, knowing that once a choice was made they could have all the exploration time they needed—but they could not quit the topic until they had worked through certain required problems. So I set some specific guidelines, but the children were free to do as many other problems as they could invent.

Derrick, who was repeating the first grade, chose the weighing center and over the period of a week he weighed just about everything he could get his hands on. He would start each day by weighing my lunch. It became a class joke; I never did figure out just why this was so hilarious, but Derrick would announce the weight in grandiose tones: "And today, Mrs. O's lunch weighs . . . " and everybody would roar with laughter. I joined in the fun by sneaking heavy things into the sack. Then, in one of those crystal moments that reminds a teacher forever why she is a teacher, Derrick decided to weigh bottle caps. Over the period of three hours Derrick made the discovery that 30 bottle caps on one side of the balance weighed the same as 30 bottle caps on the other. Can you imagine an efficiency expert letting a child persist at this for three hours? Can you imagine a child labeled, among other things, as having "attention deficit syndrome" persisting at this? The other children went to P.E.; Derrick kept weighing. This was not a problem I had set for Derrick; he came up with it on his own. About half an hour into his experiment, I realized something important was happening and started videotaping. Since I often turned the camera on and left it running while the children and I went on about our work, nobody paid any attention to it. Getting it on tape allowed me to move away from Derrick, to avoid making him self-conscious about my intense interest. In classrooms, no less than in physics, the observer changes the observed. During the three hours Derrick worked at this problem the room was busy with the activities of other children. Derrick would go "off-task" (what a whacky notion *that* is, as if children aren't learning all the time). He would get interested in a cat skeleton or the contents of a color chemistry test tube or a bridge construction project for a few minutes and then get on with his weighing. When he was close to discovery, he'd try to trick the balance, throwing an extra bottle cap on quickly or stealing one away with a very careful, light touch. Finally, he was convinced and, since my hard and fast rule was, "Write up your experiment! Explain what happened," he wrote: "30 bte cap = 30 bte cap."

The next morning, Derrick rushed into the room, ignored my lunch, and started weighing bottle caps. He quickly confirmed that 30 bottle caps still equaled 30 bottle caps. Then he confirmed that 22 = 22. He muttered, "I wish I had 1000 bottle caps." Then he weighed 1-inch cubes, confirming that 30 = 30. I should note that during this process there was a whole lot of fun when all the cubes came tumbling down. A teacher has to put up with a whole lot of mess and noise during genuine discovery. Several years later I participated in a university study on ambiguity, and, after administering their personality test, the good professors announced I had a tremendous tolerance for ambiguity. I told them it was no surprise; I'd cut my teacherly teeth on cat skeletons and bottle caps.

I have to say, too, that although my classroom, which was unique in the district and tolerated as experimental by district officials, received all sorts of commendations from my principal, from state education officials, and from parents, it was zapped after two years by a new curriculum director who moved in with her briefcase filled with efficiency schedules of what and how children should learn. That's what happens to teachers, and I think it is one reason genuine change comes so slowly. Teachers are asked to change superficially all the time, and they become good at "going through the motions." Commit yourself too wholeheartedly in what you believe in and you're sure to suffer.

I remain optimistic, however, and Derrick is the reason I do. I was Derrick's first grade teacher. Because of the funny way school districts work, I was also his seventh grade language arts teacher. We never mentioned "the good old days," but one day, overcome with a surge of nostalgia, I brought a set of test tubes to class. The seventh graders wondered what was happening. "Derrick, can you tell them?" I asked.

Derrick didn't hesitate. "You have to find an experiment, and once you find it and test it, you have to write up the results." He asked me if I had any vinegar and baking soda—and proceeded to show his classmates how to inflate balloons from the test-tube mixture. I asked Derrick if he remembered weighing bottle caps. He didn't. At first I thought, well, a teacher's significant moments are not necessarily of the same import to children. But then I realized that 30 = 30 wasn't really the point of Derrick's explorations in my classroom; he did, in fact, hold on to what really counted: Derrick remembered that he found the experiments, not me. And he remembered that writing about what happened—communicating your findings to others—is important. It is these moments that sustain teachers. I like to think they also sustain Derrick and his classmates.

Chapter

The Art of Teaching: Paradox and Passion

Baton Rouge teacher Mary Bacon knows she is fortunate to work in a district that uses its Exxon grant to expose her to new math ideas, provide release time so she can observe colleagues, send her to math conventions, provide links with the university so she can further her understanding of higher level mathematics. Clearly, Bacon will not suffer the same fate as the teacher of the math teacher in George Orwell's "Clergyman's Daughter" who leaves the school abruptly after "having been taken so badly in the middle of the arithmetic lesson." But many K–3 math specialists confess to once regarding arithmetic lessons as their least favorite activity. Marsha Copenhaver, a twenty-five-year-veteran teacher at Ocoee Elementary School in Orlando, Florida, confesses, "I hated math. That's the reason I applied to the math specialist program. I hoped it would help me improve. I knew I owed it to my students to improve."

Copenhaver admits, "When I was accepted in the K–3 Math Project, my friends and relatives laughed hysterically: 'You're going to do what?' they asked me. And when I explained I was going to become a math specialist, they laughed some more." This energetic and enthusiastic teacher obviously enjoys pulling her own leg. But then she drops her self-mocking tone and becomes very earnest: "I knew I had to get better in math because I was killing these kids with my narrow, computational view. I was the kill-drill queen. And why not? I'd had two decades to practice it. But I felt bad about my students' reactions to mathematics, and I hoped becoming a math specialist would help me find a better way."

There is almost a religious fervor about Copenhaver's conversion. "After hating math teaching for twenty-four years, manipulative materials and math journals have transformed my classroom. Now I organize my plan book around the *Standards* instead of around skill-drill." Student work fills every available space on the walls of this classroom, demonstrating how problem solving permeates these kindergartners' day:

- Which number between 1 and 10 is the favorite number of our class? Children have entered their votes on a graph and then summarized the results: "Eleven children say 10. Five children say 4. Nine children say 3."

- Estimate how many links are in the paper chain. Write your estimate in your math journal. After you count the links, write whether your estimate is "too many" or "not enough" or "just right."

- How many lunches do we have to order today?

The question "What pets do we have?" provides opportunity for another graph. The children draw small pictures of their pets and glue them in appropriate squares on the graph: "Dogs 15, Cats 10, Rabbits 2, Birds 1."

Copenhaver points out that the regularly posted estimation problem in her classroom comes from the "Estimator of the Week," the child whose turn it is to come up with something interesting for the group to estimate. "The children take this very seriously. They work very hard at thinking of a good problem and keep trying to think up more imaginative ideas." Copenhaver laughs, "I'm as curious as the children are on the morning when the new problem will be presented. One child asked the class to estimate how many feathers our bird had lost over the weekend. Another child asked how many Learninglinks we have in the room. That turned out to be complicated because the children had to figure out how to count them. They came up with a total of 564."

Samantha's journal reveals math variety and challenge in this classroom. On November 1, Samantha dictates this entry for her math journal:

I like doing the lunch count. I like making patterns using pegs. I like making high towers with the blocks. I really like doing problems— like how many more.

Not bad for a five-year-old who has been in school for just two months. Not bad, either, for a teacher who is happy to have given up her kill-drill crown.

Later in the year, the garden becomes Samantha's favorite math activity. Like her kindergarten classmates, Samantha is responsible for managing a 4-square-foot garden plot. Seventh grade volunteers help children dig, mark off their plots, and plant. This is kindergarten math with a real world emphasis.

Teachers as Learners

When asked what has brought about this dramatic change in knowledge, attitude, and teaching style as well as content, Copenhaver and her project colleagues in Orlando point to some things they have in common with teachers in schools as diverse as the Learning Center for Deaf Children in Framingham, Massachusetts; a small elementary school in a farming and agricultural community in Belgrade, Montana; a school serving a predominantly black population on the outskirts of Chicago; a school serving a predominantly English as-a-second-language and Native American population in Bernalillo, New Mexico; among others. What K–3 Math Project teachers in these schools have in common is a cooperative effort among the school district, university, and the Foundation to help reduce feelings of teacher isolation and to help teachers increase their own mathematical knowledge.

Probably the single element that sustains successful projects is that teachers see themselves as learners. Generally, these successful projects have some sort of three-part staff development program:

1. Teachers meet regularly with their peers.

2. Teachers are given the opportunity to attend professional development workshops in such topics as mathematics education, change theory, theories of intelligence, alternate assessment tools.

3. Teachers return to the university and/or the university comes into the schools for higher level mathematics courses.

This "new" professionalism means that seasoned teachers are recognizing that it may never be too late to extend their math learning, never too late to learn to think mathematically. The new professionalism takes a different shape in different projects: from teachers in Baton Rouge and Albuquerque taking refresher courses in algebra, geometry, and calculus, to teachers in Ford Heights, Illinois, returning to the university to earn master's degrees in mathematics, to teachers in Butler County,

Alabama, attending a summer workshop to learn about math manipulatives, to teachers at the Learning Center undertaking summer studies in how to make effective use of computers in their classrooms. As these teachers learn new things and thereby re-create themselves as teachers and learners, they share feelings of fear, pride, exhilaration. They talk of learning a new way of thinking.

Cognitive psychologist Jerome Bruner says that "there is nothing more central to a discipline than its way of thinking"; if teachers and their students are to become mathematically proficient, then they must learn to think like mathematicians. They must learn what Bruner calls "the forms of connection, the attitudes, hopes, jokes, and frustrations that go with it."

David Hawkins, philosopher and a founder of the Elementary Science Study, insists that subject matter for an elementary mathematics lesson must include far more than mathematics. "It should include all those things which in serious play with them contribute to children's grasping of orderings, of number and measure, of pattern and structure." Hawkins speaks of "messing about" in elementary classrooms, providing teachers and children with lots of provocative materials and plenty of time to explore big ideas.

Hawkins also insists that an elementary teacher must be a mathematician, must have at least some sense when a child's interests and proposals "are taking him near to mathematically sacred ground." Hawkins tells of a ten-year-old who noticed that in the graph he had made of area against linear dimension, the curve was locally a straight line. That child's teacher was able to support him in extensive investigations that led him in the path of Isaac Newton. Hawkins concludes, "A teacher who lacked any feeling for the calculus would almost certainly have failed him." Hawkins believes that a teacher's grasp of subject matter "must extend beyond the conventional image of mathematics." By that he means a new form, insisting "what is at stake is not the nature of the end product usually *called* mathematics, but of that whole domain in which mathematical ideas and procedures germinate, sprout, and take root, and in the end produce the visible upper branching, leafing and flowering which we here also value, and which wither when uprooted."

What It Means for Teachers to Grow in the Profession

The old saw about teachers is that some have twenty years of experience; others have one year of experience repeated twenty times. Teachers who repeat that first year again and again often seem desperate in their search for activities to keep their students occupied. Whether the mathematics activity is workbook drill or exploration with manipulative materials, the real issue is controlling student behavior. These teachers spend their careers collecting files of "What-can-we-do-Monday?" types of activities. Teachers who grow in their careers are able to move beyond the busyness of mountains of activities to a few activities that dig deeper; they learn to probe and observe a single activity for the educational significance it can reveal.

In Milwaukee, for example, a group of teachers meet once a month on Saturday mornings to share stories about what their students are doing in mathematics and to figure out how they can assess what's happening in their classrooms. They learn that just as communication is an important part of mathematics for children, it is also essential for teachers. As Susan Walter from the Fifty-Fifth Street School shares her mapping project with the group, Jean Moon suggests some questions the group may want to consider in connection with such an activity to help them develop new assessment strategies—for this and other activities:

- What mathematical behaviors are going on?
- How are the children organizing their data?
- How are the children communicating their ideas to each other?

Perhaps more significant even than the questions they are learning to ask about children's work is the fact that these teachers are meeting together. In a conversation with Bill Moyers on his television program "A World of Ideas," MacArthur Foundation fellow and educator Sara Lightfoot pointed out, "Teaching is a very autonomous experience—but the flip side of autonomy is that teachers experience loneliness and isolation. Teachers tend to miss other adult company, colleagueship, relationships, criticism, camaraderie, support, and intellectual stimulation." Lightfoot advocates "time and space in school days for teachers to come together to support one another, to respond critically to one another, and to develop plans together."

That's what Lightfoot advocates, but ask any teacher in the country; finding time and space for collegiality rarely happens.

Creating Collegiality

Terri Goyins and Earlene Hemmer taught first grade side by side at the Martha Fox Heck School in Belgrade for years without ever collaborating on anything. Then their professional lives changed forever when they heard about the Exxon K–3 math specialist grant and decided to apply. They enjoy talking about how the grant has transformed them and their community. "We had never written a grant before. We found the superintendent working in his yard and he signed our proposal then and there. We mailed it off, not really knowing just what we were starting. Later the superintendent phoned and told us Exxon had sent a check to the district for $14,000. Do you have any idea what that means in a town of three thousand people?" Goyins and Hemmer talk of the thrill of traveling to Washington, D.C., for the annual meeting of project directors, the thrill of meeting teachers from around the country, teachers with similar goals and problems, not to mention the thrill of talking with such national math leaders as Shirley Frye and Marilyn Burns. Next came their first national math conference in Salt Lake City. And, because they were now specialists, they were invited to give a workshop. "We shopped for just the right clothing, we worked hard practicing everything we could say in forty-five short minutes, we prepared wonderful visuals, and away we went. It was really scary and we decided to order two drinks sent to our room the evening before our program. The tab came to $18—you can be sure we didn't order any more." Now, a couple of years later, these two are old hands at giving workshops; they teach courses at the university as well.

These teachers, who had never worked together until they became co-directors of the K–3 Math Project, now meet every morning at 7 A.M. They also conduct monthly cadre meetings for K–12 teachers and administrators throughout the district. Goyins and Hemmer send out minutes of these meetings, both as a record and as a way to draw in other teachers. They draw in parents, too—over 90 percent participate in their Family Math Nights. If this isn't enough, these two dynamos also develop projects for weekly meetings of Math Club at every grade level in their elementary school. Topics include mental math, number patterns, measurement, geometry, calculators, tangrams, probability, fractions, large numbers, estimation, palindrome numbers, and statistics. Goyins and Hemmer are convinced that by providing teachers with provocative and accessible activities, they are spreading a hands-on, problem-solving approach to mathematics. They are helping to build a math community. Goyins and Hemmer invite their colleagues to explore math concepts in their own classrooms. They are aware that if mathematics instruction is to change, whole faculties must develop expertise rather than relying on a few "special" teachers.

Goyins and Hemmer talk of the pride of helping thirty-seven teachers move away from the textbook curriculum and toward the

NCTM *Standards*, the joy of thirty-nine teachers getting more than seven hundred students in kindergarten through the fourth grade excited about mathematics. Terri Goyins talks about how it feels to "come out from behind my desk" after seventeen years of teaching, of the new confidence she has found in herself as a professional. "My life can never be the same because of this Exxon project," she asserts. Her partner, Earlene Hemmer, also an eighteen-year-veteran teacher, was nominated to represent Montana in the national competition for the first Presidential Award for Excellence in Elementary School Mathematics Teaching in 1990 and more recently has been elected to the NCTM board of directors, the first classroom teacher so honored.

Reflection-in-Action

Franny Dever, who teaches a third and fourth grade combination class at Stapleton Elementary School in Albuquerque, reflects on what provokes and inspires change in her teaching practices. In Dever's words:

> I tend to be an action-oriented learner. If an idea makes sense to me I will dive in and try it. I have a reflective side to my nature but I usually act first, watch what happens, and revise and adjust as I go along. This style contrasts with my colleagues who are quite thoughtful from the outset; they plan carefully and predict outcomes before starting anything new. Over time, I have developed a large collection of teaching activities, but I lacked a framework to put them in. Marilyn Burns's *Math Solutions* seemed to offer that framework. She divides the math curriculum into sections: logic, geometry, number, etc. and provides a framework in which children can make choices and become responsible both for those choices and for managing their time. I was attracted by the ways math menus offer children opportunities for both exploration and responsibility. And so I jumped, head first, into math menus.

> Children showed their thinking in math logs. They could choose to work independently or in small groups on four menus throughout the year. I took the curriculum directly from the *Math Solutions* book, without much reflection on how my students would handle it. With all my educational responsibilities outside the classroom, it was all I could do to get the materials ready; I did not have time to think. Perhaps if I could focus solely on my classroom, I would have the time to plan better and be more reflective. But if I waited until I had time to "do things right," I wonder if I would ever change anything.

Many days my room looked chaotic, and my student evaluations show me that it felt chaotic to them. They complained that "math menu was confusing." Nevertheless, I could see a lot of learning going on. The students scored well on my interview assessments, on district competency tests, as well as on standardized tests.

So why wasn't Dever satisfied? Aren't good test scores evidence of good teaching and good learning? No, good test scores are not good enough for Dever. She sees part of her responsibility as working on attitudes toward mathematics and deep understandings as well as the surface proficiencies standardized tests measure. So when students tell her they are confused, she tries to dig deeper and figure out what's bothering them. One conclusion Dever reached is that third and fourth graders should not spend 50 minutes on independent work, that they need teacher response and explanation, often referred to as "mediation" in teacher jargon, as well as more opportunities to talk and share ideas with each other.

Dever explains:

If I had been working with a research team of teachers, my peer group probably could have told me the importance of teacher mediation and student sharing right from the beginning. But since I was pretty much on my own, I had to learn through trial and error. And for me this discovery represents the important next step in my growth as a teacher. For me, the move to menus was a bold move, but then I had to make it my own before it could really be successful.

Dever reports that several sessions at the NCTM conference in New Orleans helped her refine her efforts at defining a problem-solving format in her classroom.

I present a problem to the children. Then they work in pairs, solve the problem, and then present their solutions to the whole group. The children like this format. It allows everyone to enter and function at their own level of thinking. It also provides an opportunity for peer teaching. . . . I guess this is how I change, taking other people's ideas, trying them on for size, making adjustments.

Dever says that writing all this out was helpful. Usually she's too busy planning and teaching to articulate her classroom practices: her fears, problems, accomplishments, and dreams.

Donald Schon calls such musings "reflection-in-action." In his review of research at the Massachusetts Institute of Technology, Schon learned that the reflection-in-action is not dependent on previously established categories of theory and technique but "constructs a new theory of the unique case." For Dever, her classroom becomes the unique case.

Schon points out that practitioners in a variety of professions get locked into a view of themselves as technical experts. They have become skillful at techniques and situational control, and for them admitting uncertainty is a sign of weakness. Those more inclined to reflection-in-action, says Schon, "feel profoundly uneasy because they cannot say what they know how to do, cannot justify its quality or rigor," and, concludes Schon, these people need—and deserve—help in recognizing the legitimate forms of their own "professional knowing."

What's in a Title?

There is considerable evidence that the title *math specialist* carries with it the seeds of change; the title itself nurtures a sense of responsibility for educating oneself as well as others. Project directors offer similar accounts of a competent but somewhat lackluster classroom teacher who turns down offers of manipulative materials as being "too messy" and "too noisy." Then she becomes a math specialist and starts poring over professional journals and books. She transforms her classroom into several learning centers and wonders how she ever taught without manipulatives. There is lots of documentation about how math specialists grow professionally, how they sustain and support each other. Their impact on other colleagues varies, depending on how the program is structured. When the specialist offers periodic demonstration lessons in colleagues' classrooms, those colleagues don't necessarily buy into the changes in math instruction. Teachers accept the demonstration lessons but that doesn't mean they see any need to integrate the new approach or materials into their own teaching practices. I watched a classroom teacher sit at her desk and correct papers while the math specialist conducted a lesson on tangrams. In the entire fifty-minute demonstration lesson, the classroom teacher did not touch one of the seven geometric pieces that make up the ancient Chinese puzzle that teachers use to help children develop spatial reasoning skills. Nor did this teacher observe the children's strategies as they tried to figure out the puzzles. She showed no interest in the lesson. Further proof that the teacher had little interest or involvement in the manipulative approach to mathematics instruction is evidenced in the fact that every math paper on display on classroom walls was a workbook page on addition and subtraction facts. Most discouraging for any chance of change, when the math specialist finished the tangram lesson, she took the tangrams with her, so there is no possibility of further student exploration with the materials—until the specialist comes back in a week or two.

Primary schools in Orlando use a different math specialist model, providing release time for their specialists both to teach demonstration lessons and then to return to classrooms as coaches, cheering on their colleagues in their common struggle to change the way they teach. Math specialist Wini Hagy's journal reveals a pride in her own growth and in the growth of a colleague:

> I returned to the first grade where I had taught a lesson in geometry. Today I observed the teacher continue with the pattern blocks and also work at the overhead. The students displayed good retention of the previous lesson and were able to then extend their thinking while working with the blocks. I was quite proud of them! And of their teacher too.

Changing University Connections

Teachers are learning that it is never too late to become a student. K–3 Math Projects in Baton Rouge and Albuquerque sponsor higher mathematics courses for their teachers. Some teachers meet before school; others attend summer courses. Three members of the math specialist team in Ford Heights, Illinois, a district in south suburban Chicago, confess to being astounded to find themselves enrolled in university math courses; they find it mind-boggling that three of them would be pursuing a master's degree in mathematics. Especially since these teachers admit they entered the project somewhat reluctantly. Although they weren't dragged there crying and screaming, neither did Pamela Brown, Alice Mixon, Thelma Edwards, Irma Hardia, and Rhonda Johnson volunteer to become K–3 math specialists. Joyce McEwen, interim-superintendent and director of instructional programs, admits that she "encouraged" the teachers to take a risk. "Before the emergence of the K–3 math team," explains McEwen, "I would have told you that our teachers were not risk-takers."

The five teachers admit they were not thrilled to find themselves in project director Professor Lucy Chang's university math course. They are quick to acknowledge that Chang's high standards were tough to live up to, particularly after a long day in the classroom. The teachers were tired and worried they wouldn't be able to cope, but Chang soon pulled them in with her enthusiasm, her fire, her determination—her insistence they could think mathematically. Pamela Brown says that Chang "wouldn't let us give up on ourselves or our students."

Chang reminded the team, "I've been in your district, I've seen the extreme need for mathematical understanding." Chang told the teachers and their administrators that "without mathematical knowledge and skill, it is nearly impossible for teachers to be creative. Without mathematical knowledge, you can be creative in the wrong ways. Cute," insists Chang, "is not necessarily creative."

"Conceptual learning must precede procedural understanding or 'methods,'" insists Chang, and it is this premise that made her course so difficult for the participants. Chang would teach a class, teachers would write a lesson based on the theoretical construct of the class; then Chang and her university team went into the classrooms and observed the teachers as they conducted that lesson. Finally, teachers would return to Chang's class at the university and talk things over. Ford Heights teachers admit that at first they were impatient with the theory, impatient that they weren't getting paste-and-take, prefabricated lessons. "We wanted cute," they admit.

These teachers take pride in poking fun at their former selves; they also take pride in acknowledging the difference Lisa Chang has made in their lives. Chang is quick to return the kudos. "These teachers walk proud. They started out as primary teachers thinking they couldn't survive a math course. But the power of colleagues helping each other to take risks and grow together has changed their professional lives. Now they are not intimidated by math; they are pursuing master's degrees." Chang smiles and adds, "And they are influencing their peers. Other teachers in District 169 are asking for university courses. They insist they want me to teach them everything that I taught the Exxon group."

From remaining isolated in their building to attending the NCTM convention in New Orleans, these teachers talk about how far they have come professionally in a very short time. Nominated by her peers, Pamela Brown, first grade teacher at Medgar Evers School and new master's candidate at Governors State University, received the South Suburban Math Council Award for Excellence in Mathematics Teaching. This teacher, who had never been to a professional meeting or had any contact with professionals outside her district, is now accepting invitations to give workshops; she travels to national conventions. "We've been to a national convention," she notes, "we can go anywhere and do anything."

As important as Chang's influence has been, she echoes Sara Light-foot's comments on the necessity of colleagueship for lasting change in teacher behavior to occur. Chang is quick to point out that the crucial element in these teachers' change is not a professor changing a teacher but the teachers' own professional network: five teachers changing one another, not one teacher trying to do it alone.

Eleanor Duckworth observes that the rare teacher can take the leap into a new way of teaching all on her own on the basis of a book she reads or a course she takes. Most teachers, however, need the support of some nearby colleagues who are trying to make the same changes. Joan Good-man, first grade teacher in the Albuquerque K–3 Math Project, observes, "I think all teachers are at risk. Getting together and talking about common plans, hopes, fears, and dreams reduces that risk."

Teachers (and professors) are learning that teacher education and reeducation is wonderfully complex and that the road to the university need not be a one-way street. In Montana and Baton Rouge, for example, K–3 math specialists are invited to the university to teach pre-service courses and courses on the *Standards*. A collaborative program between the University of New Mexico and the Albuquerque school district moves an experienced teacher from the public schools to the university for two years. Patty King, formerly a K–3 Math Project classroom teacher, is now a clinical supervisor with student teachers at the university. During this time King will supervise student teachers while they work with children; she will also team teach with the university professors in the mathematics methods block of courses. After two years King will return to the classroom and another teacher will become a clinical supervisor.

King, a classroom teacher for thirteen years, takes her reflections on her own growth as a teacher into the university. She says that when she moved from teaching in a kindergarten literacy program to first grade about five years ago she felt secure and creative in all areas except math. "I pulled out the workbooks and said 'work in your books,' day after day." King notes that although she was not comfortable with all the workbook pages, she "simply did not have the resources to change, nor even the time to think about how to change."

King reflects that although she wondered if the students had any notion of why they practiced computation on hundreds of workbook pages, "it is difficult for a teacher to give students what she never had." Since mathematical understanding had never been a part of King's own education, she did not know how to bring understanding to her classroom. Nonetheless, that small doubt, that niggling worry that workbooks might not be educationally sound, did not go away:

I had no experience to draw from. I didn't even remember having a methods course in mathematics education. My own school experience was one of math anxiety. I clearly remember cheating on my third grade multiplication test where we were supposed to have our times tables memorized. Throughout my schooling, math continued to be memorizing formulas and doing lots of problems for homework and taking tests for which there was only one answer. I hated it. I could memorize, but I could never understand what I was doing. I did well in high school algebra but dropped out of geometry, convinced that I wasn't smart enough for it. And that was the end of my math career.

Learning from One Another and from the NCTM

King points out that her strong background in early childhood education saved her as a first grade teacher. "I knew about graphing whether kids rode the bus or walked to school, if we preferred chocolate or vanilla ice cream. We measured and recorded the growth of plants, ran a play store or a restaurant with play money." Then King teamed with another teacher in a first and second grade combination class. "My teammate had read Constance Kamii's *Children Reinvent Arithmetic* and brought Kamii's strategies into our class. We used lessons based on Math Solution videotapes made by Marilyn Burns, the calendar math from *Math Their Way*, games from *Box It or Bag It*, and anything else that made sense. At last I had someone with whom I could talk over lessons and assess students' understanding. The constant professional dialogue was essential to my growth."

King attests, "I could never 'go back.' My growth has been developmental; it has come in stages and has been inspired in part by not wanting to teach the way I was taught and knowing in my gut that the textbook is not enough. I want my students to become empowered with the confidence that they can solve problems." King's classroom is "alive with discourse as students explain their thinking." She believes that students are risk takers unless someone convinces them to be otherwise. "From watching my students engage themselves and then express that confidence, I have come to believe strongly in the constructivist idea that the understanding is constructed within the individual (not poured in from an external source). Memorizing and rote learning do not contribute to understanding. Teaching according to the NCTM Standards does."

Maria Variegas Coleman, teacher at the Pueblo Gardens Elementary School in Tucson, also draws on her own pain as a student to illuminate her work as a teacher, recalling that she flunked geometry twice because "the very traditional, rote memorization of facts" in elementary school did not prepare her to understand the underlying mathematical structures. Coleman notes, "I persisted, but by the time I finally passed geometry I was math phobic and afraid to try higher math in college." Coleman is grateful that the K–3 Math Project helps her join with colleagues to learn all she can—about mathematics and child development—so she can provide a different environment for her kindergartners, to get them asking questions and explaining their own thinking rather than spouting back meaningless numbers they've memorized.

Carol Brooks, mathematics specialist and director of Chapter 1 Mathematics for the Tucson schools, uses the Exxon grant to give Coleman the opportunity to meet in grade-level meetings once a month with her colleagues to talk about teaching and learning mathematics. They bring their students' work and discuss individual children as well as groups; they share the latest research on how they might best evaluate student work; they also share lessons on integrating literature and mathematics. Such meetings are noteworthy both for their value and their rarity. Most teachers in the United States never have a chance to talk about their students with colleagues—unless they forgo phoning parents, using the copy machine, tutoring children who need extra help, and the many other activities they try to crowd into their twenty-seven-minute lunch break—and then are able to find a colleague who is also willing to forgo all of the above in order to chat.

In my own twenty years of teaching, only once was I invited to a meeting with colleagues from other schools in my district who taught the same grade as I did. At that one meeting, one third grade teacher from each school in the district was called to a central place to vote on a textbook recommendation. I found our textbook wrangling stimulating and informative. But our recommendation was later overruled by the elementary coordinator. On another occasion, I filed an application to take one of two professional leave days guaranteed in our contract to observe another third grade classroom in my district. But the district assistant superintendent in charge of curriculum denied my request as "frivolous" and of "no clear professional benefit." Too many schools are like mine rather than those in Tucson. In too many school districts, professional benefit is seen to accrue only by traveling at least fifty miles; in such districts experts are people who arrive by jet.

To get real value from the experts, a district must have an ongoing structure for teacher growth in place. It must provide a nurturing environment for the contrasting styles of teachers like Dever and King.

Where King takes the broad view, seeing a steady, positive development in her professional growth, Dever zeroes in on a particular classroom problem, worrying and nudging it. Both teachers are helped to gain control of their professional lives because they work in a system that nurtures and sustains them, a system that gives them opportunities to talk and study with their colleagues. They are, in short, treated as professionals.

The Way It Is Supposed to Be

The simple fact of the matter is that teachers who are not treated as professionals often fail to grow professionally. They often drop out—or hang on desperately to what becomes a thankless, routine job. They become plodders who do the same exact job year after year, using the same workbook pages (or the same Unifix cubes; manipulatives don't come with fail-safe guarantees any more than textbooks), looking neither to right nor left to assess the needs of the children. More often than not, these teachers will insist they teach what they teach and the way they teach because that's what the district and state mandate say they are "supposed to teach." And yet, next-door colleagues, working under these same mandates, teach very differently. Rexford Brown points out that mandates don't constrain all teachers; teachers constrain themselves by their degree of professional development.

Jerome Bruner says that each of us has to construct our own version of reality; for teachers that means each of us must create the teacher we are. We are capable of re-creating ourselves, learning new things, though it isn't easy. Glenda Stone, a twenty-five-year-veteran teacher at the W. O. Palmer Elementary School in Greenville, Alabama, confesses that she was nervous when confronted with learning a new approach to teaching math. She notes, "I'm a structured person, and this seemed unstructured. But then I realized that the other structure belonged to the textbook; it didn't have anything to do with the mathematical structure—or with how children learn." Stone notes that she and her students are having a lot more fun in math these days. "This is a lot more fun than workbooks—for the children and for me." She tells her principal, "I can't do this in an hour. I may need two hours." She asks him to back off and be flexible about schedules, noting "when people believe in teachers, teachers produce. They are saying we can take charge of our curriculum—and we can."

Stages of Change

Teachers who do grow as professionals often go through five stages:

1. *Ain't this fun!*
   The teacher relies on the textbook for her content, her bulletin boards are filled with skill-drill worksheets plastered with "Good work!" stickers. This teacher may have a "free math" time once a week for the children who finish their workbook pages. A major shift for this teacher is to drop the workbook.
   When asked to share a lesson, this teacher sends an AIMS lesson or other commercial black-line master—without adaptation.

2. *I'm doing Math Their Way (or AIMS, Box It or Bag It).*
   This teacher adopts ideas outside the textbook but moves through the alternative text without alteration—so that despite palm trees and 75-degree weather outside, her first graders graph their favorite snow activities because *AIMS* has snow activities. This teacher becomes expert at implementing someone else's program and takes delight in the new, fun experiences this program brings to her students. Because becoming a disciple of these programs requires a lot of preparation (all those kidney beans to paint), the teacher may confuse busyness with virtue and even ideological purity. A plus is that children are likely to become involved in hands-on projects.
   When asked to share a lesson, this teacher might send an enthusiastic narrative about children graphing jelly bean colors—or snowmen.

3. *I'm doing Burns.*
   This teacher has begun to read more widely and is beginning to see her students as informants for her classroom practices and procedures. Her planbook is much less likely to be neat and tidy—with lessons fully spelled out ahead of time. She is aware of—and perhaps seeking membership in—the larger mathematics community.
   When asked to share a lesson, she is likely to send her variation of the cows and chickens problem, adapted to the interests and backgrounds of her students.

4. *I'm better than Burns.*
   This teacher has integrated the ideas of others into her own belief system, a belief system that she has only recently been able to identify clearly. She uses these ideas as starting points for her own reflection and curriculum building. She is taking school knowledge and making it her own. She is probably reaching out to unmet colleagues through articles and/or workshops.

When asked to share a lesson, she sends a stack of her students' journal entries.

5. *I'm not just a teacher—I'm a researcher.*
This teacher is actively reflecting on her teaching in order to expand theory in the larger mathematics community. "How?" takes a distant second place to "Why?" in her lesson plans. An active member of the professional community, she is at risk of "moving on"—out of the classroom—unless her district can find ways to sustain and nurture her growth. If she hears too often that she's "wasting herself" in the classroom, she may start to believe it.

When asked to share a lesson, this teacher sends a stack of her own journal entries or an article she's written.

Of course these categories are not mutually exclusive. They overlap, intertwine, and sometimes don't fit a given teacher. More importantly, a teacher at Stage 5 carries with her traces of Stage 2. Teachers do, after all, continually face the question, "What will I do on Monday?" And teddy bears and jelly beans do have their appeal. Most importantly, there is no virtue inherent in any stage. Teachers do what they have to do and what they can do.

The Summer of 1989

I developed the above stage theory before I heard about what happened the summer of 1989 in Las Cruces, New Mexico. I feel I have to explain this because what happened in Las Cruces seems to have so well encapsulated the paradoxical stages of a teacher's development—but I don't want Las Cruces teachers to think what happened that summer is unique to them, and I made up a chart to describe their professional angst. Their confusion and ambivalence were squashed into a unique summer of intense training, but their reactions are typical of teachers everywhere.

During the summer of 1989, K–3 math specialists in Las Cruces studied under the guidance of three very disparate mathematical theories. Dr. Walter Secada of the University of Wisconsin presented Cognitively Guided Instruction (CGI). Teachers complained from the start that Secada was "too theoretical, not practical enough." Not to worry. Las Cruces was in for a summer of teacher training. Next came a *Box It or Bag It* workshop. It would have been popular in any case, but, coming after what the teachers regarded as a highly theoretical presentation, the teachers were ecstatic. This is what they had been waiting for. In Marian

Pelking's words, "This is what teachers thought being a math specialist was all about: working on 'Make It and Take It' to bring back to your classroom and then 'Share It' with colleagues. K–3 math specialists worked incredibly hard for five days, trying to make as many of the math manipulatives in this program as they could. A note to business and industry: you don't know hard work until you've seen a teacher making hands-on materials for her students. Teachers invested a lot of time and money in the diverse materials that it takes to implement this program. They were buried in Con-tact paper, storage boxes, Milar mirrors, posterboard, laminating paper, Gummy Bears, miniature marshmallows, toothpicks, paper plates, Baggies, popcorn kernels, and so on and so on.

Teachers filled the workshop with "oohs" and "aahs" as each new thing was created and as each clever new variation on a theme was displayed. Teachers didn't work just during the workshop; they worked at a frantic pace day and night to create enough *Box It or Bag It* materials to get their students off to a good start at the beginning of school.

But then came the next teacher training workshop. The first week of August, Constance Kamii gave a two-day, sixteen-hour workshop on her Piagetian/constructivist vision of how children invent their own arithmetic, demonstrating in vivid terms that children must create their own understanding by solving problems with other children. Kamii informed the math specialists that they did not need "all of that junk" they had just so laboriously put together. "What children need," stressed Dr. Kamii, "is time and space to play mathematical games with other children. If they are to learn to solve problems, to construct mathematical concepts that will serve them in the future," insisted Kamii, "children need intense interaction with other children." In short, they don't need gummy bears.

Teachers were furious. They attacked the workshop planners for the lack of continuity among presenters. "At least you could have put the workshops in the right sequence," complained one teacher, "so I wouldn't have wasted all that time and money making junk."

K–3 Math Project directors Karin Matray and Marian Pelking assured teachers that if they liked their *Box It or Bag It* materials, they should indeed use them. Matray and Pelking decided a fourth workshop was in order. They tried to pull things together in a six-hour session, reminding teachers that the most important concept stressed by Secada, Kamii, and the *Box It or Bag It* presenters is to observe children at work in the classroom. Teachers can choose what they observe children doing—be it CGI problems or Gummy Bear sorting or a Kamii-style game—but the important thing is to observe the children and to let that observation inform their instruction.

As school got underway and teachers settled into their routines teacher comments about the summer workshop began to take a new turn:

- You know, I kind of see what Dr. Kamii was talking about. I was really upset when she talked to us, but now I listen to and watch the children in a different way. I am amazed at how much math the children already know.

- I tried rephrasing some of the math problems like Dr. Secada suggested and he's right. I had been using just one form of math problem and now I am trying other ways.

As Marian Pelking talked with teachers, she noticed that once they had some time and distance from their summer of disequilibrium, they seemed to be excited about everything they had learned. And they were anxious to learn more. Most important, they took charge of their own training; several attended a Marilyn Burns *Math Solutions* workshop the next summer at their own expense. Pelking notes that after the initial intensive, and perhaps contradictory, summer of training, "Teachers seemed to realize they have to make the very real, hard choices themselves; they can't hire their pedagogy from a consultant." As Matray and Pelking reflect on that first summer, they have come to the conclusion that teachers applied initially to the K–3 Math Project not because they saw themselves as learners, but because they saw themselves as good math teachers. The training they received in the notorious summer of 1989 forced them to evaluate their own teaching belief systems—and to challenge themselves both as teachers and learners.

Sharing Significance

When I first started working on this project, I sent out a letter to teachers: "Please share with me your significant classroom anecdotes, terrific lessons, and anything else you can think of." Nothing happened. Part of this is because teachers' lives are so jammed—they simply don't have the time to write up classroom significance. But there is more to it. Another part of the difficulty lies in the fact that, for good teachers, a "lesson" is not a single, finite thing (except on the days they are being evaluated under the Madeline Hunter or similar behavioristic plan) whose beginnings and endings can be clearly marked off. And there are even larger concerns, ones that get to the heart of being a teacher:

1. Teachers are reluctant to call attention to themselves and say, "Look at me. Am I not terrific?!!"

2. Teachers torture themselves with self-doubt. As Albuquerque project director Lois Folsom said, "They self-tyrannize, constantly asking themselves, 'Am I good enough? Am I worthy?'" The better the teacher, probably the more anguished the ambiguity she sees in everything she does. There's always that sense of missed opportunity, of wishing she'd done more. Aware of all the possible contradictions and alternative paths, she never feels she's taught that perfect lesson. (The upbeat side of this is that good lessons never reach closure; there's always more.)

3. Teachers acknowledge that they borrow from their mentors, and despite all the adaptations and additions, despite the unique ways in which they respond to the needs of their students, they feel they "own" the lesson only in terms of their own classroom—not in terms of sending it off to someone like me.

Like a Möbius Strip and a Garden

The practical idealism of the classroom is filled with paradox. Lots of classrooms have all the "right" manipulatives but they also have stacks of skill workbooks. Many teachers are not about to put all their eggs in one tub of pattern blocks any more than they put all their faith in one textbook. For all the upbeat enthusiasm of successful teachers, there is also a grayer quality that's hard to pin down, a needling, persistent, lingering whisper: "E. D. Hirsch and John Saxon may be right, and you may be wrong." Only the underdeveloped teacher is ever convinced she's right all the time. For the savvy teacher, the craft is ever like a Möbius strip, filled with internal contradictions. In exploring how being awarded a K–3 math specialist grant has affected teachers, I have seen every range of behavior. I've met teachers who are naive and teachers who are sophisticated, teachers who were waiting for this "excuse" to change as well as teachers who are still trying to hide from change. To explain what I mean by "excuse," I would point to the remarkable convenience and security inherent in a teacher being able to link her decision to delay the teaching of multiplication algorithms to the fact that she is participating in a grant from a gigantic, well-respected entity such as the Exxon Education Foundation. Principals, parents, and the media are considerably more reluctant to give a hard time to a math specialist working under such an aegis than they would be to the typically frazzled teacher who doesn't have a business card or letterhead stationery. I am sure that a lot of school district leaders are unaware of the radical transformation in mathematics going on under their very noses simply because they would never dream of questioning anything with the weighty credentials of big business.

Michael Pollen says that a garden is never finished. Neither is a schoolroom. Because the people who comment on educational policy and practice are not the sort of people who closet themselves for 182 days a year with a room full of eight-year-olds, few people outside the inner circle have any notion of what this calling is all about. People figure the schoolhouse has no mysteries because, after all, we have all spent a lot of time there. The teacher teaches and the children learn: so what's the fuss all about? Unlike doctors and lawyers, teachers don't even have a mystery language with which to befuddle the public. But we teachers are survivors. We need a motto of the "neither storm nor sleet ..." type. What outsiders never guess and insiders rarely confess is that teachers who triumph develop a good dose of what Keats called "negative capability"—the ability to exist among uncertainty, mystery, doubt, insult, affront, and indignity. They work in difficult conditions, they nurture the children in their care. I have visited a great variety of classrooms across this country, and I can testify about the teachers who tend them: they are resilient, adaptable and tough. They will persist and endure.

Chapter

Teachers and Administrators: Learning and Working Together

The sign on the principal's office at the Garfield School in Milwaukee, Wisconsin, reads:

Dr. Kery Kafka
Head Learner

It is a powerful message for students and their teachers. I am moved by that sign; I stand and stare at it for a long time.

Cheryl Johannes, a principal in Belgrade, Montana, describes her leadership style: "I just try to get out of the way." But when her students are involved in the Math Olympics, Johannes is very much in the middle of things. Donning a hat that says "PRESS," Johannes carries a video recorder and interviews students. "What do you think about these Math Olympics? What about the problem? Has your group come up with a strategy?" Although teachers are clearly in charge of the event, this principal's enthusiasm is contagious. When a reporter and camera crew from a local television station show up, all the children agree that Johannes asks better questions than the real reporter. Part of Johannes's definition of "getting out of the way" is to do away with first grade achievement tests in her school. One spots the gleam in her eye and wonders how long it will be before other achievement tests bite the dust. She also has made sure that every teacher in her building receives *Math Their Way* training. "I want teachers who can articulate a whole language belief system, and I won't hire anyone who doesn't have this

157

training," insists Johannes. She adds, "Of course the most important quality in teachers I hire is a positive attitude about children. But I want to be sure that they also have a belief system that can deliver the curriculum in an integrated way."

Cheryl Johannes is anxious to talk about what wonderful teachers staff her school. After launching into an animated description of a graphing lesson she'd witnessed in Terri Goyins's first grade classroom, Johannes recalls, "All the children were talking and sharing information about graphs. I had goose bumps three inches high!"

Let Sleeping Principals Lie

Another principal offers a telling contrast that becomes evident from the moment I introduce myself. Despite the fact that I have made an appointment and explained the purpose of my visit, he asks, "Now just what are you here to see? Oh, math," he laughs. "Well, I'm sure you know more about it than I do. I was never good in math." In contrast to most schools I visit, this principal does not inundate me with stories of what a wonderful job his staff is doing. Instead, he comments on the weather as he guides me to the classroom of the math specialist, saying, "I'll leave you here. Ms. ——— knows a lot more than I do about what's going on in math." He is laughing; the math specialist isn't.

Certainly some teachers would be grateful for such a principal. Benign neglect is preferable to interference. Every teacher has a horror story of working under the gun of an administrator who can't give up any control, who doesn't want things to change, who feels very threatened by teachers' emerging expertise and the assertiveness that comes with expertise.

A number of math specialists report that administrative noninterference is the best support they can expect. As one specialist put it, "We have a tacit agreement: my principal is pleased that I have the initiative to go after things like this Exxon grant; he neither knows nor cares anything about it, but he's smart enough to know that my initiative makes him look good." This teacher notes that although the principal is very traditional, he supports the use of manipulatives in classrooms because she reminds him, "Exxon wants this." She isn't the only teacher I meet who knows how and when to use the corporate name. This K–3 math specialist feels good about being in a position to make sure that every primary classroom in her building is "loaded with manipulatives. . . . My principal's disinterest has made me powerful."

Another specialist observes, "The administration here is asleep. They have no understanding that a radical change is taking place under their noses. The funny thing is that they just assume that because this project is sponsored by Exxon, it must be safe. You know, big business surely wouldn't do anything radical." She laughs. "That's fine with me. For me, a sleepy principal is a good principal. And I use the Exxon name a lot to keep them sleepy and content." Another teacher agrees, adding, "I am grateful that my principal values me enough to find a way to adapt our district's behavioristic evaluation system to my classroom style." She pauses for a moment, "I guess I'm dissatisfied because I want him to be aware of what's happening in education, to share articles with me, to understand the changes I'm trying to make in my teaching. That's what I want, but I settle for a whole lot less. Isn't it ironic that we consider this principal 'good' because his sins are of omission rather than commission? Nonetheless, I am grateful that he lets me run my classroom the way I want."

Do As I Say, Not As I Do

When I notice that Madeline Hunter, renowned proponent of a tightly structured lesson that is turned into a checklist evaluation system by many administrators, is scheduled to give a workshop for the K–3 specialists in a district, I ask how Hunter's philosophy aligns with the goals of the math specialist project. Suspecting, no doubt, that I might be one of those people for whom Hunter's name is a red flag, the supervisor is defensive. "Madeline never said there should be seven steps . . . and teachers do need to know where they're going . . . they have to be accountable." My experience in schools has taught me that when an administrator says teachers need a ready-made structure in order to make sense of their teaching, it is usually the administrator who needs that convenient, prefabricated structure in order to make sense of what's going on in classrooms. Significantly, as this administrator guides me through the K–3 classrooms, he calls no student by name; neither do any students call him by name. Quite a contrast with Tucson and Albuquerque and Orlando, where administrators are frequent classroom visitors. As soon as these "supervisors" enter a classroom, they start teaching; they know the children and the children know them.

Later, at a meeting with the teachers, I can't resist bringing up Hunter again. "How does the Hunter teacher evaluation system line up with your goals as K–3 math specialists?" Immediately there is an explosion of resentment; sarcastic comments like, "How would you like to fit an exploratory lesson with manipulatives into the anticipatory sets framework?" Someone else jumps in, "And closure. Don't forget closure." It is clear that this issue, one that cuts to the bone, has never been raised in the K–3 monthly meetings. All that palpable antagonism has remained submerged. The teachers seem relieved that someone has finally asked this nasty little question, has acknowledged the fact that the teacher evaluation system runs contrary to the environment of exploration and discovery outlined in the NCTM *Standards* and ostensibly promoted by the very administrator whose job it is both to head the math reform movement in the district and evaluate the team of reformers. As one teacher says later, "If you don't trust teachers, then you set up this supposedly fail-safe curriculum system and you evaluate teachers by checklist." She pauses and then adds, "And destroy their souls."

In private, several teachers tell me of oppressive evaluation "criteria" that penalize a teacher if a student looks away from the teacher while she is talking. In the jargon of the trade this is "engaging in off-task behavior." Teachers lose points on their evaluation if students ask "inappropriate questions" or make "inappropriate remarks." One teacher muses, "Can you imagine what happens to your evaluation score when you have an independent, creative student in your class—a future Einstein or an Edison?" Yes, I can. I know of more than one district where colleagues babysit disruptive or "independent" students while their teacher is being evaluated. There are all sorts of ways to beat the system, but in this kind of system, there are no winners. Everybody loses.

I am puzzled by the fact that these same teachers who express such resentment over the form of their evaluation also had the good fortune to attend several staff development courses led by well-known leaders in mathematics education. During my three-day visit in their classrooms (including a four-hour staff meeting), no teacher mentioned her life being touched by these leaders. Only one teacher even referred to any of the math leaders or the courses they had taught in the district. I wonder if, when no cohesion in philosophy exists and evaluation runs contrary to instructional goals, an intellectual community can flourish. And if there is no community identity, I wonder if any outside luminaries can have much of an effect on teachers' belief systems. Furthermore, it is doubtful that teachers who don't see any possibility to change insulting portions of their working conditions can be effective change agents for their students.

The Carrot-Stick Ethic

If teachers are evaluated by a behavioristic model, many of them will bring this same philosophy into their classrooms. "Control" becomes a much bigger issue than curriculum content, and a carrot-stick ethic is prominently displayed on classroom walls. Students are reminded every minute of every day that certain behaviors are rewarded and other behaviors are punished. One school posts the behavior carrot-stick system on a bulletin board outside the principal's office:

POSITIVES	NEGATIVES
certificate	Warning; name on board.
awards	+ lose recess
stickers	++ lose recess; call parents
party	+++ lose recess; call parents; conference with principal

This same chart is predominantly displayed in classrooms throughout the school. It is then no surprise that when I ask a second grader why he is working with Unifix cubes, he tells me if he finishes the stack of task cards his teacher is going to give him a McDonald's certificate. Even with prodding and broad hints, I cannot pull from him any other purpose for engaging in this activity. Finally, I ask, "How long is it going to take you to finish?" The seven-year-old rolls his eyes, shrugs, and heaves a huge sigh. He seems to be on the edge of realizing a great truth: a hamburger couldn't possibly be worth all this work. Unfortunately, nobody is encouraging him to consider that mathematics just might be a rewarding pursuit in and of itself, that you don't need to be bribed to do it.

Give Every Teacher Business Cards

Orlando K–3 Math Project leader Linda Levine says, "If you ask your staff to change, then you must support them with high quality in-service, and you must give them support every step of the way." Teachers may not have believed it in the beginning, but one form of support offered by Levine and her math resource team is the math journal. K–3 math specialists are expected to keep journals in which they reflect on:

1. Their mathematical knowledge.

2. Their refinement of good teaching methods and strategies.

3. Their students' subsequent reactions.

As I read some early journals, I can see the specialists' awareness of Levine's high expectations. These teachers know they are expected to join a larger professional community: to read professional journals and books, preview new materials, and otherwise increase their math expertise.

In Orlando, teacher change is supported in very specific ways by administrators. Each math specialist is given some trappings that business professionals take for granted but are unknown in most faculty rooms: a subscription to the *Arithmetic Teacher*, letterhead stationery, and business cards. Specialists are also sent to professional conferences, invited to present workshops within the district, and involved in making decisions on everything from line items in the budget to classroom materials to curriculum. After seeing the spirit and pride produced by Orlando's very deliberate efforts to treat math specialists as professionals, my recommendation to every board of education in the country is to provide business cards for their teachers.

During a budget meeting in Orlando to cut costs, math specialist Felicia Ryerson suggests that she would rather relinquish extra pay for extra work than give up attending professional meetings, which she considers necessary for her professional growth. Leanna Isaacson, a principal and member of the budget committee, is just as impassioned in her plea that teachers "not be asked to work for nothing." Voicing her worries about teacher burnout, Isaacson insists, "You can't drain people forever. We have to find someplace else in the budget to cut. It can't come from the teachers."

Administrative Guidelines That Encourage Teacher Reflection

Keeping a journal is not easy for many of the teachers—one more thing to worry about in a busy day. Many are obviously not used to reflecting about their craft, particularly not in writing—and especially knowing these reflections will be read regularly by supervisors. Typically, teachers begin their journals by "reporting in" on current reading. They log in their journals how much time they spend reading—with no mention of content other than the titles. Operating in new territory, these teachers are clearly anxious to know, "Am I doing enough?" They don't voice this worry directly, but administrative staff members who read their journals pick up on the anxiety and write back quietly reassuring comments. Gradually specialists begin to read and write for themselves, for their own growth, and not because somebody is checking. What starts out for many as a duty becomes reflective.

When teachers are practicing what Albuquerque project director Lois Folsom refers to as "self-tyranny," the administrator can make a marginal comment to the effect, "Give yourself a break." When Sandra Young, Orlando math specialist, confesses in her journal that she doesn't know enough about fraction manipulatives, she receives this administrative reassurance in the journal margin: "Lighten up; you've only been a math specialist for two weeks."

Young's journal reveals what an important event the NCTM convention is for a group of teachers who have never attended. She begins talking about the convention in her journal half a year before it takes place. Young admits she is excited but also "Petrified!" about the reception the Exxon Education Foundation is holding for K–3 math specialists from around the country at the convention. The reader can sense Young's apprehension about how she will measure up to her counterparts from around the country.

Young's journal documents the level of administrative support her district provides to help her change the way she teaches mathematics. During her first six weeks as a specialist, Young notes in her journal that she has watched the six Marilyn Burns videos on manipulative materials, read Burns's *The Good Time Math Event Book*, and attended workshops on Cuisenaire rods, calculators, visual imagery, and problem-centered learning. Young proudly announces that she has moved the individual student desks out of her classroom and brought in round tables so that her students can work in pairs. Three weeks later she reports, "I took all my workbooks and tests and put them in the closet."

From the Mouths of Babes

Orlando administrators send another important message about what matters when they require all math specialists to conduct individual, taped interviews with their students about their math attitudes. Children also take more traditional types of end-of-the year math tests, but, clearly, an administrative team that asks students how they like to do math and what uses they see for math is trying to align assessment goals with teaching goals. If we say that math is a humanistic endeavor, then we need to ask students' opinions about that endeavor. Here are some representative responses:

"What do you think about students helping each other solve math problems?"

- I'd rather work by myself because I'm too smart. (kindergarten)
- I do things quicker by myself. (kindergarten)
- I like working with other kids because you can work faster. (kindergarten)
- Good idea. (first grade)
- Happy. It would be too hard for just one person to do it. (first grade)
- I like it because you're being friendly and it makes them feel good. (first grade)
- I like helping other students, because sometimes you make friends. (first grade)
- Good. Because you can help other people out. (first grade)
- Good. Because when somebody needs help, somebody needs to help them. (second grade)

"When do you use the math you learn?"

- Sundays and Fridays. (kindergarten)
- When you need to. (first grade)
- When the teacher tells you it's time to do math and you have to do what the teacher tells you to. (second grade)

"How do you learn math the easiest? What things or activities help you learn it better?"

- Base-ten blocks. (third grade)
- Unifix cubes. (kindergarten through third grade)
- By writing about it. (kindergarten through third grade)
- With friends. (kindergarten through third grade)
- Calculators. (kindergarten through third grade)
- Pattern blocks. (second grade)
- Listening to the teacher. (second grade)
- Skill sheets. (third grade)
- When I ask my mom. (third grade)

"Why do you have to learn math?"

- Because. (second grade)
- Because the school tells you to. (third grade)

A number of kindergartners said you have to learn math so you can be ready for first grade. Anna expanded on this theme: "Because we're young and we have to learn lessons or we can't go into first grade." Charles said, "If you know math, you don't have to stay in kindergarten; you go to first grade."

And why do first graders learn math? "So then you can go to second grade." And for second graders, "Math is important when you go to third grade. They're gonna ask you about math." A third grader said, "It's good for your brain," but another third grader said, "Because there's a lot of math in fourth grade." Seven-year-old Timothy said, "When we get to high school they might ask us some math problems," and seven-year-old Katie said, "You need it in college." But seven-year-old Kelly gave this bottom-line answer: "Every time you get in a grade, you're going to be doing math. When you go to work, they'll ask you if you did math in school." And Jamie put a cap on the question by responding, "So you can help your kids with their homework."

These children agree with Lynn Arthur Steen, whose celebrated book *On the Shoulders of Giants* refers to the "layer-cake approach to mathematics education," an approach that "reinforces the tendency to design each course primarily to meet the prerequisites of the next course, making the study of mathematics largely an exercise in delayed gratification." Instead, insists Steen, we need to build curricula with greater vertical continuity "to connect the roots of mathematics to the branches of mathematics in the educational experience of children." Steen advocates "multiple parallel strands, each grounded in appropriate childhood experiences." This means that mathematics is no longer regarded as being constructed from separate sequential skill chunks but that children are exposed to multiplication while they are still learning addition; students don't wait until tenth grade for geometry but start learning it in kindergarten. And when they get to tenth grade they will no longer study geometry in isolation but throughout high school will take courses that integrate algebra, geometry, and trigonometry.

The teacher who sees these kinds of responses from her students is reminded to embed "reasons" for math in her curriculum, reasons that range from the poetical to the practical. Children in one first grade reveal they are aware of the potential of mathematics. These first graders say they study math "because it makes you smart; it's good for your brain; you can grow up to be a construction worker or a doctor if you know math." Six-year-old Horace announces, "So I can be a mathematician. When you do math, it's called mathematician." Christopher generalizes, "Because it's good to learn things," and Tramaine replies, "If you don't know how to learn math, that means you don't want to learn nothing."

Teachers and administrators look at these responses—and they learn from them. For one thing, they ask themselves what did this one teacher do that made her first graders' attitudes about mathematics so different from those of most other primary graders?

Looking for the Fire in Their Eyes

How does a school district help teachers keep the spark of enthusiasm alive? Jay Hoffman, assistant superintendent of educational support services for the sprawling (100 square miles) Temecula Union School District in Temecula, California, and project director for the district's math specialist grant, suggests starting the way you want to proceed. "I look for the fire in their eyes during the initial interview," says Hoffman. "I don't want people with massive egos, but I want people who are confident in themselves and their ability to take charge." Hoffman credits a pro-teacher school board that "believes in micromanagement instead of top-down policy-setting with maintaining good staff morale." And, asserts Hoffman, "All the strategies and all the materials in the world won't do you any good if you don't have good staff morale." Hoffman talks of the district commitment to send ten teachers to the NCTM annual conference, noting that a teacher feels very special to be in the midst of 24,999 other conferees who care a lot about mathematics. For most of these teachers, it will be their first time to attend a national convention of any kind. "The first time," affirms Hoffman, "to feel really professional."

Part of the Exxon grant for Temecula Valley concentrates on training student teachers in primary math education. Known in the jargon of the trade as *pre-service training*, this training is done in conjunction with San Diego State University and the University of California at Riverside. The Riverside campus has established a teacher center at one of the elementary school sites. Hoffman has convincing evidence that teachers are revitalized by training student teachers. At any given time, eight to ten student teachers and a university supervisor are assigned to the site, and Temecula Valley teachers work with them. One of the benefits of such a collaboration, observes Hoffman, is that the district has an opportunity to preview budding teacher talent—to spot those prospective teachers with fire in their eyes. In an effort to narrow the traditional gap between what student teachers get in their university training and what district personnel and the teachers themselves perceive they need in the classroom, the Temecula project offers pre-service teachers a seminar series taught jointly by university and school district faculty. Each participating pre-service teacher receives a stock of manipulatives—to help her start off on the right foot wherever she might end up teaching.

Getting Children out of the Classroom and into the Parking Lot

Pat Yavno is principal of the Vail School. Built in 1965, it is one of the older schools in the Temecula Valley District, a district that has exploded in size in recent years. Yavno's attendance at several Marilyn Burns *Math Solutions* courses with a dozen of her teachers reflects her determination to be a curriculum leader. She describes Burns's "wonderful pragmatism" as very suited to her own style, one she seems to infuse throughout her building. A strong advocate of math manipulatives, Yavno led a drive in her school to gain $12,000 in state school improvement funds for the purchase of manipulatives. The next year they wrote a curriculum plan to buy a calculator for every student in the school.

There is a consistent, widespread breadth and variety of student investigation in this school, paying tribute to strong and informed leadership; even Halloween pictures in the hallway have a math flavor.

- In Joe Campbell's third grade class, one child is measuring another child's foot while a small group plays a money game.

- In Ms. Hoen's fourth grade class, children are trying to predict the average number of seeds in an apple. They have written a hypothesis: "We do not believe that the size and/or weight of the apple will make a difference in the number of seeds in the apple." They are working on a procedure statement, and the teacher reminds them that scientists also write abstracts of their work.

- Blanche Raye and her kindergartners are not in their classroom, and Yavno is pleased rather than surprised. "Education shouldn't be confined to one room," she comments. We find the kindergartners out in the parking lot, where Raye is reminding them,

How Many arms Do the mummies Have in the Counting Creatures? — Shayla Johnson

Halloween mathematics in Temecula, California.

"Estimation means 'take a good guess.'" These kindergartners are estimating how many cars are in the parking lot.

- Primary math specialist Liz Morris's second graders are writing in their math journals, explaining what they've been doing with their calculators. In a district that has seen a great influx of newly hired teachers, Morris, like other math specialists in the district, is trained to be a mentor to these new teachers as well as consultant to the veteran staff. And she has been trained for this role. Unlike teachers in some districts, Temecula math specialists don't have to read the manufacturers' labels to figure out which end of the manipulative is up. They are sent to training sessions before they are expected to use the materials in their own classrooms and coach colleagues in their use.

Helping Teachers Realize That What They Have Is Time

For Lois Folsom, director of a K–3 Math Project that includes urban Albuquerque and nearby suburban and rural Bernalillo and Las Lunas,

New Mexico, effecting and supporting change is at the core of the project. This project focuses on the change strategies for success identified by the Rand Corporation:

1. Concrete, teacher-specific, and extended training.
2. Classroom assistance from project or district staff.
3. Teacher observation of similar projects in other classrooms, schools, or districts.
4. Regular project meetings that focus on practical problems.
5. Teacher participation in project discussions.
6. Local materials development.
7. Principal participation in training.

Folsom comments on one practical problem they have addressed. "Teachers often say, 'If only we had more time,' but we realized that in actuality, what teachers have is time; it's how we choose to use our time that counts." One strategy Albuquerque uses is to pair upper grade and primary teachers. Teachers then combine their classes regularly, thus freeing one teacher to lead a study team. And students benefit directly from the mixed-age learning.

Another unique aspect of the Albuquerque project is to place two math specialists at a school. Folsom believes the mutual support these pairs have been able to give one another, particularly in the beginning, "gives them an incredible strength of resource and support to effect change." Folsom insists:

All of us are change agents by doing what we say. We don't just talk about it; we do it. This means me; this means the teachers. We're trying for bottom-up, unsponsored, gentle change. We have twelve Exxon teachers modeling and demonstrating a different way of teaching math, reaching out to individual classrooms in their schools. If it is going to work, these individual teachers must be the major force which provokes change in their schools. One way we try to help them administratively is to recognize that no two of our teachers are alike. We accept this difference. In fact, we celebrate it. We don't want our classrooms to look alike. Whether you are talking about teachers or students, for learning to take place, you have to have ownership. You have to process it through your own value system. . . . One major thing the teachers have in common is they self-tyrannize all the time. They are constantly asking themselves—and me—"Am I good enough?"

Loy Sue Siegenthaler, a consultant who has worked extensively with the Albuquerque project, talks about how the group is very egalitarian, "much more invested in the common good than in any idiosyncratic needs." She says project teachers worry a lot about their own personality styles, about being too pushy in their efforts to influence other teachers in their schools. Siegenthaler also talks about Folsom as leader. "In the beginning the specialists kept trying to force Lois to make decisions so they could react, but she'd turn it around and ask, 'What do you think?' Because of Lois's style, some teachers had to relinquish some of their own power." Siegenthaler points out that some groups take two years to resolve this control issue; the Albuquerque teachers did it in two months. She points to the tremendous amount of affection that has resulted, the sense of camaraderie and cohesion.

Folsom insists, "I don't take responsibility for knowing everything. There is plenty of room for everybody to know lots of things." It is no wonder, then, that Las Lunas math specialist Joan Goodman can say, "Do you know how powerful I feel?" Anyone who is not astonished by Goodman's assertion should try asking ten teachers at random how powerful they feel.

Learning Together

Over the past several years, Rexford Brown, a senior policy analyst for the Education Commission of the States, visited schools across the country where "thinking and problem-solving activities were supposed to be a major part of the curriculum." He concludes that although in every school he and his team visited "someone knew what to do and practiced it to some degree," rarely would he describe the majority of teachers in a school as practicing thoughtfulness. Brown concludes that the most developed districts have created more thoughtful environments for the adults in the system. In these schools, says Brown, "Adults are visibly engaged in inquiry, discovering, learning, collaborative problem solving, and critical thinking." Brown adds that "anyone who hopes to excite and challenge young people without exciting and challenging their teachers hopes in vain."

Brown's conclusions may seem obvious but they are rarely practiced; few districts have shown themselves capable of creating thoughtful environments for the adults who work in them. I have, however, seen districts working hard at creating this thoughtful environment. During the summer of 1991, Lois Folsom helped the Albuquerque group of math specialists push themselves to a new level of information and involvement by taking a higher math course together. Siegenthaler observes that the risk of enrolling in this difficult course "generated a new sense of confident competence in the teachers." Folsom also sent all the Albuquerque math specialists to the NCTM 1990 national convention in Salt Lake City and again in 1991 to the conference in New Orleans. Teachers who attended these conferences talk about a degree of bonding that outsiders find hard to fathom. In math specialist Joan Goodman's words, "It was a most exciting time—a whole week to think and browse and talk about math."

The Orlando project also sent their teachers to the conventions, and the importance of these conventions was evident when the Orlando district planning team met to hammer out a budget. They soon discovered their dreams exceeded the monies available and began looking for places to cut. Sending the project teachers to the national convention seemed to be the most obviously expendable item—until Felicia Ryerson, math specialist and the teacher representative on the committee, spoke up. "You can take away our extra money for planning time, you can cut back on supplies; don't take away support for conference attendance. I would never have gotten to Salt Lake City or New Orleans on my own, and until I'd been I would never have guessed what being at a national conference could mean." Ryerson points out that it's one thing to read articles by leaders in the field and quite another thing to hear them in person, to be able to listen to the audience's questions—and ask your own, to sit in the same row with luminaries at the presentations of other leaders in the field. "For one thing," notes Ryerson, "you always think you are the only person who doesn't understand something; you always think your questions are probably dumb. And there at the convention you see half a dozen people asking the same questions you wanted to ask. Who would ever guess that the experts would have the same questions? Ryerson adds, "Besides the stimulation of close encounters with mathematics experts, I had a week of very intense talking and sharing with my own colleagues. Where else would I ever have such an opportunity to learn and reflect and connect with teachers?"

Anybody who is surprised that a teacher might have to travel from Orlando to Salt Lake City to have an in-depth conversation with a teacher in her own district does not understand the degree of isolation experienced by teachers. Although the K–3 Math Project is breaking down the barriers that produce this isolation, the fact of the matter is that in most districts across the country it is far easier for a teacher to obtain permission to attend an out-of-state conference than to visit a colleague's classroom in her district—or even in her school. Many districts stipulate "two professional days" in the contract, but everybody knows that when you take a professional day, you are supposed to get on a plane.

Creating Thoughtful Environments

Carol Brooks, math specialist and director of Chapter 1 Mathematics for Tucson, uses Exxon grant funds to make sure that administrators and teachers learn and work together to create thoughtful environments. "You can't send teachers off to learn new things and just hope the principals will catch on; they need to learn new things together so they can support one another." Brooks sets up specific guidelines for schools to use Exxon funds to attend Math Solutions courses. First, at least five teachers from a school must attend together. Second, their principal must attend with them. "This means that teachers and administrators alike will have a support system in their building that they can keep coming back to."

Lois Folsom agrees. "If you want change to occur, such a support system is absolutely essential. Going to a convention or taking a course together gives people a bond; they maintain and build on that connection after they return to their schools. Each Exxon teacher can draw on her membership in the larger Albuquerque group while maintaining her own small intraschool group too."

In the summer of 1992, thirteen Tucson administrators attend the Math Solutions course, nine for the level three course. There is heavy competition for available slots, with over two hundred teachers and principals on the waiting list for the beginning course. Admission to the level three course is by invitation only, and Brooks initiates a contract: all teachers who attend the level three class must agree to assume a mathematics leadership role when they return to their schools.

Evidence that creating a thoughtful environment over time is having its effect, that it is creating change and maybe even an education revolution, can be seen in the recent decision of the Tucson school district not to buy mathematics textbooks. Principals and teachers decided that rather than spend over $1,000,000 on a textbook adoption, they would invest in a variety of teacher and student resources.

Training in a Soap Factory

School districts use Exxon funds in many different ways, but all successful K–3 Math Projects have the same core emphasis. In contrast to many reform movements of the past, these excellent projects make teachers the center of the curriculum. They depend on classroom teachers to rescue mathematics and they acknowledge both that teachers come in many shapes and styles and that teaching is not a neat and tidy craft.

James Q. Wilson writes about what he calls the "kooky efforts to bureaucratize teaching." Wilson points to a 1910 report by an efficiency expert commissioned by the Carnegie Foundation for the Advancement of Teaching. This expert recommended that university professors use standardized lecture notes in order to make universities more productive. A commentator of the time said that the expert's report "reads as if the author received his training in a soap factory." Any educator in the profession more than half a decade can point to personal encounters with similar soap factory attitudes. Wilson observes that more recent reforms intended to get schools "back to the basics" grow out of a distrust for the authority and expertise of teachers; ironically, the fate of these reforms ultimately depends on teachers, the very people who are so reviled and distrusted. Savvy administrators who want to reform mathematics education are trying to learn a lesson from the soap factory reform movements of the past; they acknowledge that teachers are the only hope.

Chapter

Parents: Partners, Not Problems

Exxon project teachers laugh as they recall the first night of Family Math training at the Medgar Evers School in Ford Heights, Illinois, a suburb of Chicago. "We made them fix their own refreshments, asking for 'guesstimates' for preparing punch," recalls Alice Mixon, first grade teacher and math specialist at the school. "They argued about whether they could change their number; they 'counted on' while pouring cups; we talked about 'reference point' in estimation. One father guesstimated how many sheets of paper towels it would take to reach across the room. Then everybody watched him count them all—and cheered him on." Family Math Nights have become the stuff of legend in this community. Mixon and her project colleagues, Irma Hardia, Rhonda Johnson, Autry Arbor, and Pamela Brown, talk about the parent who showed up at a math session the night after her house burned down, commenting, "This is too important to miss." Another parent who went through the Family Math program has gone back to school, training to become a teacher's assistant. Indeed, parent education in the types of mathematics that are revolutionizing primary graders' classrooms was so well received at Medgar Evers that it has spurred the formation of a Parent Teacher Organization at the school.

Parental involvement is a crucial component in most Exxon K–3 Math Projects, and math specialists aren't satisfied with the traditional definition of parental involvement: a good turnout at open house.

Knowing that parents are the single most influential factor in their children's attitudes about school, K–3 math specialists want to bring these influential people in as partners in the changing mathematics curriculum. For starters, many math specialists structure programs to explain and demonstrate the NCTM *Standards*; they want parents to understand the day-to-day classroom practices that are very different from the good old arithmetic of "Readin', 'Rritin', and 'Rithmetic" so well known to past generations. Specialists also expose parents to the theoretical underpinnings that drive these new classroom practices, holding parent workshops to give parents hands-on experience in activity-oriented mathematics. These specialists send home newsletters and plan PTA programs—both to explain what's going on in the classrooms and to suggest how parents can offer support with activities at home.

It Ain't Necessarily So

One thing teachers and administrators are learning is not to believe their bad press. Educators who believe what the media and the politicians dish out are likely to perceive the public as the enemy. Teachers have become inured to bad news about schools; they know from experience that good news usually evaporates before it leaves their individual classrooms. People who work in schools may have every right to feel paranoid, but they are learning that the undifferentiated, anonymous mass known as "the public" is very different from the parents of children in their classrooms; teachers and administrators are discovering that parents are their best allies. In point of fact, the public takes two stands on American education. When asked a broad question about the state of education in this country, the public responds that the schools are bad, even deplorable. But when the focus is narrowed and this same public is asked about the individual schools their own children attend, their judgments change dramatically. The closer people get to home, the less likely they are to rely on and quote from global pronouncements from editorial writers, television commentators, and politicians about the failure of American education. The public quotes SAT scores and the fact that American kids don't measure up to Japanese kids on a fifth grade mathematics test. In contrast, parents quote how well their children can figure things out, how inventive they are. Parents who are intimate with a local school don't base their judgments of that school on newspaper headlines of impending national disaster resulting from SAT scores or on pronouncements from blue ribbon panels. People with insider knowledge of a local school are still likely to make sweeping denunciations of other people's schools but are very likely to be positive about the own child's classroom. Parents have insider knowledge of the schools their children attend; they get this knowledge from talking to their children, their children's teachers, and other parents. They have day-to-day interactions with classroom practices over a very long period of time. Parents are not as narrowly focused as media sound bites would lead us to believe. Yes, parents care about skills, but they are also very much attuned to the affective elements of schooling. Achievement test scores are one small part of parent concerns; they also want to know if their children like school, if they are risk-takers, if they are cooperative, creative, self-motivated, and persistent. According to a 1988 Gallup Poll of the public's attitudes toward public schools, only 25 percent of the responding parents give the nation's schools a rating of *A* or *B*. But when these same parents are asked to grade "the school your oldest child attends," 70 percent give these schools top marks. In a 1990 Gallup Poll, although the total of *A*s and *B*s given to the nation's schools at large fell to 21 percent, the grade given to the school where the respondents' oldest children attend crept up to 72 percent.

What would a baseball team owner offer someone who hit .720? Teachers and administrators need to know that plenty of people think they are doing something right.

Family Math: Learning New Things Together

Even though the K–3 Math Project's participating schools in Baton Rouge, Louisiana, are different from schools in Belgrade, Montana, and Tucson, Arizona, and Framingham, Massachusetts, one important thing these schools have in common is Family Math Night. Originating at the Lawrence Hall of Science at the University of California, Berkeley, the Family Math program operates from the premise that when children and their parents learn mathematics together in a nonthreatening, supportive environment, math skills improve in significant and lasting ways. According to Nancy Krienberg, director of the Family Math program, "It doesn't take more than a half hour for parents to see that they're not going to be in a situation where they will have anxieties." K–3 Math Projects use the book *Family Math* as a guide to a hands-on activity approach to mathematics. Collaboration, with lots of talk and sharing and experimentation, is encouraged in Family Math workshops. Family Math focuses on parents and their children "doing" mathematics together, especially problem solving. Family Math trainers are very specific in what they mean by problem solving:

> We mean ways in which people learn how to think about a problem using such strategies as looking for patterns, drawing a picture, working backwards, working with a partner, and eliminating possibilities. Having a supply of strategies allows a choice of ways to start looking at a problem, relieving the frustration of not knowing where to begin. The more strategies you have, the more confident you become, the more willing you are to tackle new problems, and the better problem solver you become.

Changing Math Requires Changing Communication with Parents

The reaction of a parent from Irvine, California, who attended Family Math sessions is typical of parents around the country: "I dreaded going. I would never have believed that math could be fun. But it can be and it is. I wish I'd had math like this in school." This parent did not talk about how her and her eight-year-old's mathematical problem-solving ability measured up to that of mothers and eight-year-olds from other parts of the country or to that of mothers and eight-year-olds in Japan; rather, she talked about mathematics being not only doable but actually fun. This woman who had regarded herself as a mathematics dunce since the fourth grade now talked about a new realization that she could have a positive effect on her child's ability in and enthusiasm for mathematics.

It is not surprising that in a planned community like Irvine, where 115 homeowners' associations hold the final word on everything from the color of one's house to the height of one's geraniums, people would also be vigilant about what's going on in the mathematics classes in their local schools. From the beginning, Irvine schools have been organized around a model of limited diversity, or site-based or school-based management, operating within an administrative framework of overall unity, a sort of maximized collective freedom, meaning that schools in Irvine are more the same than they are different. And they have extensive grade-by-grade *Curriculum Management Guides* to make sure they stay this way.

Irvine school officials care a lot about keeping their parents happy, and they have enough confidence in their own delivery system to believe that an informed parent is a happy parent. All Irvine schools that applied for an Exxon Education Foundation grant to establish K–3 math specialists brought parents into the grant planning right from the beginning. Although parents are routinely included as a natural part of the goal-setting meetings that take place in Irvine schools, when a curriculum revolution such as the one taking place today in mathematics is underway, parental involvement takes on added importance. With the California State Education Department outlining mathematics goals that include the removal of the times tables from the third grade curriculum, the Irvine Unified School District's decision to create a district-wide parent education program in mathematics this past year can be seen as just plain savvy public relations. Parents who help school personnel set the curriculum goals are likely to be allies of that curriculum. And when you're talking about eliminating sacred rituals such as memorization of the times tables, you know that you're going to need all the allies you can get.

The K–3 Math Project had added appeal for the Irvine school community. They already had long experience with teacher specialists in music, art, and science; mathematics seemed like a logical next choice. Since Irvine schools are organized around the principle of site-based management, six different schools submitted five different math specialist proposals (two schools collaborated on one proposal and they share one specialist), each tailoring an implementation plan to meet its own specific needs.

Dr. Dorothy Terman, curriculum coordinator for the Irvine Unified School District, looks to the five teachers designated as K–3 math specialists to design their own plans for keeping parents in their schools informed about and involved in mathematics. Most schools conduct "needs assessment" surveys in the fall and then reassess in the spring to see how they've done. Significantly, parent needs get equal billing with those of teachers and students. Believing that "an enhanced student enthusiasm for math" will emerge when parents understand what the math program is all about, Terman is eager to talk with math specialists about their individual plans for getting parents into the schools on Family Math Nights.

Nancy Vaughn, math specialist at Brywood School, a school whose students come from homes with a diverse socioeconomic span ranging from government-subsidized housing to $450,000 single family dwellings, points out that negative math attitudes cross all socioeconomic backgrounds. Vaughn points out that negative feelings about math are so pervasive that parents don't see any need to pretend they like math. She reports, "When I asked parents at the Family Math meeting, 'How many of you like math?' no one raised a hand. Nobody."

Not liking math, however, does not keep parents away from four Family Math Nights at Brywood. And they come away with the surprised realization that mathematics has undergone dramatic changes from their own school days. Vaughn also keeps in regular contact with parents through *Math News*, a parent newsletter. The newsletter provides a brief explanation of the theoretical base of something such as problem solving as well as offering age-appropriate problems and projects parents can try with their children. Vaughn also supplies a math page for the principal's newsletter that goes home to parents each month. Here's the January offering from the *Brywood Bugle*:

"Look! Math Ideas to Use While Riding in a Car."

- Count from 0 to 9 using digits seen on license plates. (counting, digits)

- Read license plate numbers. (numerals)

- Add all the digits on license plates and record each sum. Find as great a sum as possible. A calculator could be used. (adding, calculator usage)

- Compute mileage for a trip. Estimate beforehand from a highway map. Also estimate the amount of fuel needed. (estimating, adding, dividing)

- Add points for the things the children see. Children collect points for different animals they see: birds count 1 point each; dogs, cows, and cats, 5 points; horses, 10 points; a cat in a window of a car, 100 points, etc.

- Other versions: establish a point system for makes of car, different vehicles on the road, signs seen, or types of buildings.

Brywood and Santiago Hills Elementary Schools held a "needs assessment" survey. Parent focus groups consisting of a random sample of eight to twelve parents were formed. Parent moderators led the group in a discussion of parent attitudes about mathematics programs and practices.

Among the focus group questions asked of parents were the following:

1. What do you see from your child's class or hear from your child that lets you know what your child is doing in math?

2. What growth, if any, have you noticed in your child's math ability?

3. What, if anything, would you like the school to provide you with to help you work with your child in math?

4. When you think of math, what comes into your mind?

5. With or without your help, how much time do you think is reasonable for your child to invest in math homework per week?

6. Do you feel that calculators should be used? How? When?

7. Would you support a math facts program similar to the weekly spelling program?

Randomly selected students were also asked their opinions about every area of their math curriculum as well as more general questions such as:

1. Why do we study these topics in math?

2. How do grown-ups use math?

3. How do you use math at home?

4. What do you like to play at home?

5. When you think of math what comes into your mind?

6. What is your favorite thing about math? Why?

7. What is your least favorite thing about math? Why?

8. What sorts of mathematics would you like to do? That you would think are fun?

9. How do you think you will use math in the future?

Student surveys reflect a national trend: the higher the grade, the less favorably students view mathematics. Like their parents, students focus only on the numeration part of mathematics. Survey results convince curriculum developers to increase their emphasis on the understanding of mathematics and the role it plays in real-world applications.

Site-based management allows Irvine schools with different needs to offer different programs. At the Culverdale School, for example, 45 percent of the students were born outside the United States, but school staff do not allow language and cultural differences to become an obstacle to parental involvement. When Culverdale parents were polled about their concerns, teachers found that among the greatest parent concerns was not a feeling that their children lacked basic mathematics skills but rather a feeling of their own inadequacy in helping their children achieve excellence in mathematics. Acting on this information, school personnel invited parents in for a math orientation meeting early in September and send parents newsletters to keep them informed of math happenings in the school. The PTA held one of their meetings in the school math lab so that parents could see both the room and the materials their children were talking about. In addition to providing parent and volunteer training, the school maintains a mathematics resource library for parents.

Because the El Toro Marine School serves the children living in military housing at the El Toro Marine Corps Air Station, with 98 percent of its population being Marine dependents, transiency is a major consideration. School personnel make special effort to make parents who know they will be moving before long have a sense nonetheless of belonging to the community and the school. Math specialist Josette Marculuso uses a page in the *Principal's Newsletter* as a way to make parents aware of the NCTM *Standards*. Feeling the importance of helping parents get a sense that math is "universal" and not particular to a classroom or a school, Marculuso discusses one standard each month, supplementing this explanation with a description of what students are doing in classrooms and offering suggestions for ways parents can support this learning at home. Early in the year Marculuso helped plan a PTA meeting devoted to math manipulatives. By explaining the rationale behind the use of manipulatives and letting parents themselves experience the hands-on appeal of these materials, Marculuso feels parental suspicion about changes in math instruction will be forestalled. Parents at El Toro Marine supported a five-week Family Math parental training program in the fall and another series of sessions in the spring. The El Toro Marine PTA bought manipulative materials for the school.

Ironically, Irvine school personnel interpret a high approval response from parents as proof of the need for parental education. For example, when 90 percent of the parents at Springbrook Elementary School expressed approval of the traditional, textbook-based mathematics program, the school staff instituted a program of informing parents about the *Standards*. They set about informing parents about the need for curriculum change in three strands in their school: logic, measurement, and geometry.

Quilting Experts Are Math Mentors

Surveying parental attitudes also plays a crucial part in the planning stages of the K–3 Math Project in Jackson County, Kentucky. When a parent admits, "I thought math was just figuring with numbers," curriculum planners listen. This is a county where 78.5 percent of the children are judged economically disadvantaged by the index of qualifying for free lunch. In a county where only 25 percent of the adults over the age of twenty-five have high school degrees and 17 percent have less than five years of school, a county with the highest dropout rate in Kentucky and the third highest dropout rate in the nation, project leaders have made parental involvement the key ingredient in their struggle to restructure primary grade mathematics.

Knowing the parents might feel intimidated by the idea of getting involved in any kind of mathematics in the school, Judy Sizemore, schools programs coordinator for the Appalachian Communities for Children and also coordinator of the K–3 Math Project, recruits parents to become involved in an art project. Although Sizemore's underlying goal is the development and reinforcement of math concepts, she doesn't feel she needs to announce that fact to parents right up front. Very aware of the discomfort many parents already feel in the schools, Sizemore feels announcing a mathematics agenda would just add to this discomfort—and probably keep people away.

And so Sizemore brings math in through an already existing Parent Art Council. Sizemore said, "It is easier to recruit parents for an art project than for a math project. We designed art projects that would reinforce math concepts." Thus the construction paper quilt project is born. Parents in eastern Kentucky know about quilts; they feel comfortable with their expertise, know they have information and skills to contribute. Being asked to contribute to a construction paper quilt project gets the parents into the school, and before long both parents and students discover that they are learning simultaneously about math, art and local history. Before the parents come in for the quilting project, students become familiar with pattern blocks in their math classes. Parent quilters are given some initial training and learn certain terminology, so by the time they visit classrooms they can talk with children about how they create their quilt patterns from geometric pieces.

Parents are surprised and delighted to know that they have been working with math all their lives. "I thought math was just figuring with numbers," said one mother. "I never thought about math in the garden or in my quilts, but now I see math everywhere."

After they have talked to real quilters from their community and seen demonstrations from these quilters, students work with pattern blocks to create an original quilt design that they then reproduce in construction paper. Parent volunteers prepare the construction paper copies of pattern block pieces ahead of time so that they are available for student work. Students experiment with geometry patterns and glue the designs they like onto construction paper backing. Parent volunteers then laminate these "appliqué blocks" so students can continue using them for a variety of mathematics activities. Later, children are challenged in a more advanced project to create quilt blocks where the pieces themselves must form perfect squares of a particular size. One class decides to make a quilt of hexagonal blocks; they quickly become enmeshed in lots of discussion about fractional parts and trapezoids. Students soon realize that to make the triangles visible they need to be careful in their color choice; math again becomes aligned with such artistic principles as complementary and contrasting colors.

In a nation that is becoming increasingly obsessed with such mathematical "outcomes" as standardized test scores, schools like those in Jackson County thus makes a deliberate decision to tap into the uniqueness of their own community, training parents to return to their roots as a way to inspire and rejuvenate mathematics in their children's classrooms. The benefits of mathematical quilting are readily apparent to students, teachers, and parents alike. Parents who have always considered themselves "bad at math" see that they had very definite skills to share with the children, skills of academic value. Talented needle artists discover that they have been applying important math concepts for years without even knowing it. A number of parents express the view that this kind of math, a math that emphasizes community skills and values at the same time it encourages students to broaden their horizons, might do for children what it couldn't do for their parents—keep them in school. The quilt project is one of many activities in Jackson County in which parents are recruited—and trained—to bring specialized mathematical knowledge into the schools, thus turning the tables somewhat on the traditional teacher-as-expert addressing parent in role of inadequate supplicant. The Appalachian Communities for Children project uses its Exxon grant to make parents the experts. The numbers tell a tale. At the end of the first six months of the project, about 15 percent of the parents in the district had played an active role in the project and roughly 50 percent had responded in some way to the monthly newsletters and phone calls made by project staff. By the end of the year, 50 percent have played an active role in the project and 80 percent have responded to the newsletters and phone calls.

Sizemore credits a visit to another K–3 Math Project in Pulaski County with cementing this strong parental cohesion. Impressed with seeing the activity-based *Box It or Bag It* mathematics in action, the Jackson County group immediately purchased this teacher resource guide. Sizemore organized the parents to make all the materials needed for the calendar activity. Sizemore notes, "Parents were delighted to see the excitement and enthusiasm of the teachers when they brought in the calendar manipulatives all ready to go; parents began to feel that they were playing a critical role, making a genuine contribution."

Twenty-Two Teachers and Multiplying . . .

Schools in Laurel County, Kentucky, with economic statistics similar to those of Jackson County, also makes a top priority of active community involvement in the way mathematics is taught to their children. Cheryl Chedester, K–3 Math Project director for Laurel County, made an appeal to the Younger Women's Club in London, the county's largest city with a population of 7445. The Younger Women's Club adopted the K–3 Math Project as their core community involvement project for 1990, donating $1800 for the purchase of Unifix cubes and teacher resource books for every elementary center in the county. Then Chedester and her team trained twenty-two K–3 teachers, representing the eleven elementary centers, in the use of the Unifix cubes. Chedester is enthusiastic. "Those twenty-two teachers went forth and multiplied. They went back to their schools armed with a variety of lessons using Unifix cubes to teach number sense, place value, multiplication and division, measurement, area, perimeter, logic, and problem-solving skills." Chedester points out that the teachers are enthusiastic about sharing new techniques and concepts with their students and their peers. Chedester adds, "Of course we communicate with the Younger Women's Club to let them know of the phenomenal impact of their generosity, but they get the word very directly, too, as their own children and their neighbors come home and tell them about these exciting things called Unifix cubes."

K–3 math specialists in the Hillsborough County Schools in Tampa, Florida, contribute ideas to Math Link, an eight-page math newsletter filled with activities, resources, letters asking for advice. One page is directed to parents, giving both specific suggestions on how they can help their children in the mathematics of the 1990s and a brief rationale of why this help is so essential.

When kindergartners at the Forest Hills School in Tampa were given the opportunity to write books for their mothers for Mother's Day, even their teachers were surprised when the children spontaneously decided to tell their moms how much they like mathematics. Kyle draws

KYLE

In Tampa, Florida, a kindergartner draws himself engaged in his favorite activity (sketched from the child's original art).

In Tampa, a kindergartner makes a Mother's Day card, a self-portrait showing off her graph (sketched from the child's original art).

a picture of his hand making a graph and writes: "My favorite part of kindergarten is whenever we graph." Chantel draws herself triumphant, graph in hand: "My favorite part of kindergarten is graphing." Danielle shows herself standing beside graphs. Other kindergartners report such activities as measuring pumpkins and spinning the circle as their favorites.

Changing the School's Relationship with Families

In the second volume of his memoirs, *What Do You Care What People Think?*, Nobel physicist Richard Feynman recalls the strong influence his father had on his development as a scientist. Feynman's father would read to him from the *Encyclopedia Britannica* that the height of, say, tryannosaurus rex was 25 feet:

> My father would stop reading and say, "Now, let's see what that means. That would mean that if he stood in our yard, he would be tall enough to put his head through our window up here. But his head would be too wide to fit into the window." Everything he read to me he would translate as best he could into some reality.

Feynman concludes that his father "started very early to tell me about the world and how interesting it is." K–3 Math Project teachers hope to honor and stimulate this kind of parental influence and involvement in their children's mathematics education. Take a look, for example, at Las Cruces, New Mexico. Located about forty-five miles north of the Mexican border, Las Cruces is one of the fastest-growing metropolitan areas in the nation. The ethnic composition of the nineteen elementary school is about 52 percent Hispanic, 46 percent Anglo, and 2 percent other. Over half of the students qualify for free and reduced lunches, but socioeconomic levels and parental education backgrounds are widely divergent. As well as being the home of New Mexico University, the area hosts many scientific and technological jobs. In designing their K–3 Math Project, the Las Cruces team gave major consideration to helping teachers recognize the changing family structure and differing relationship with the school of even the so-called traditional family of the 1990s. Dr. Diana Del Campo of the New Mexico State University Cooperative Extension Services, a family life specialist involved in research and training on the changing nature of parent involvement in education, helps math specialists identify new and different ways of involving parents in their children's education. Teachers are encouraged to move from an old model of seeing the parent as someone to do something for the school to a model of the school as an institution that can help the parent.

Since communicating with parents and keeping them informed of what's going on in the schools is designated a top priority for the Las Cruces project, a newsletter, *Math Fiesta: Celebrating Math at Home and School*, was developed as a vehicle both to explain how the teachers are receiving special training to meet the nation's mathematics needs of the twenty-first century and to make suggestions of how parents might support these efforts. The first edition of *Math Fiesta* briefly explained that twenty-eight Las Cruces teachers have been trained to be math specialists and that their training includes:

- the use of math manipulatives;

- how to build better computational skills;

- how to include math in other subject areas;

- how to use writing skills in mathematics;

- the use of computers and calculators.

Knowing that it is especially important for parents to understand the "legitimacy" of methods of instruction that are very different from when they went to school, this first issue linked the teacher training with a brief explanation of how this training fits what's happening at the national level, the NCTM *Standards*.

Stressing the theme "Math is everywhere! Enjoy it with your child!" *Math Fiesta* shows parents that helping their children to think mathematically is something every parent can do; it requires neither special materials nor torturous skill drill. *Math Fiesta* demonstrates that inspiration for mathematical thinking is all around the house—everything from sorting kitchen items to estimating time intervals with the kitchen timer to counting blue cars while traveling. One edition of *Math Fiesta* offers suggestions on ways parents can make snacktime fun as well as educational; it also offers ways parents can use that irresistible concrete object—money—to help their children to think mathematically.

ESTIMATION

How Many M & M's in the Bag?

Put some M & M's (or raisins, Cheerios, etc.) in a small bag. Have your child guess how many you put in the bag. Have your child write down their guess (or you write it for them) to help enforce place value concepts. Then, empty the bag and help your child count out the M & M's. Separate the candies into groups of 10 by sorting them on a flat surface. Count the 10's first and finish with the ones (10, 20, 30, 40, 41, 42, 43, 44). Compare the actual amount with their estimate. For older children, find the difference between the estimate and the actual amount.

How Many Licks to Eat a Popsicle?

First, decide with your child just what exactly is a lick, then have each child estimate how many licks it will take for them to eat a Popsicle. This is difficult because no bites are allowed! Write down the estimations, then have your child start licking. Determine how you want to keep the official count. Older children may want to keep track of licks by marking tally marks on a piece of paper. When finished, compare the actual licks to the estimation.

How Many Seeds in a Piece of Watermelon?

Give your child a piece of watermelon to look over. Have your child estimate how many seeds are in that piece. Again, write down the estimate. Set the seeds aside as your child eats the watermelon. When finished eating, count out the seeds, sorting into groups of 10. Again, compare the actual number with the estimate. No fair eating extra seeds to make the answer come out closer!

MONEY

Children love money! Making $10 worth of assorted change available to your child is the cheapest math manipulative you can find. Try these money activities:

Using the weekly grocery store ads, ask your child to select food items for a particular meal. Have your child count out the amount of money necessary to make the purchase. Children love to cut out

Grocery mathematics in Las Cruces, New Mexico.

the pictured items and paste them on a separate piece of paper, writing down the amount of purchase.

What Can I Buy?

Put some small items (candy, stickers, erasers, animals, etc.) in small plastic bags. Give each item a price tag. Tell your child that he/she can buy as many items as he/she has money for and help your child as he/she counts out the cash. This can be done several ways—your child can pay for each item separately until all the money is spent; your child can use paper and pencil to add and/or subtract as he/she buys the items; your child can use a calculator to help total the purchases.

Spelling Cents

Play a money game with your child's spelling list. To find out how much each spelling word is worth, add up the value of each of its letters using this formula: a = $.01, b = $.02, c = $.03 . . . z = $.26. For example, the word "house" is worth $.68.

$$h = \$.08 \quad o = \$.15 \quad u = \$.21 \quad s = \$.19 \quad e = \$.05$$

This is also a fun game to play using children's names, vocabulary words from social studies or science, street and city names, etc. Great game for in the car or waiting for an appointment.

Math specialists Pam Waugh and Sam Hoffman provide a special parent page for the end-of-the-year *Math Fiesta*. Explaining that first graders have been involved in daily calendar math work all year, they provide tips on how parents can extend these activities during the summer, emphasizing numeral recognition: counting by ones, twos, fives, tens; number combinations ("How many ways can you think of to make this number?" We call this "incredible equations"); and problem solving ("If grandma can stay for 5 days, what day will she leave? If we must be back on the 24th, how many nights can we stay on our vacation? How many days until school begins?").

Public schools in Wichita, Kansas, have developed interdisciplinary thematic units to disseminate an integrated math curriculum in kindergarten through the third grade. These units include a parent information component, a home activity kit created by the math specialists. Here are sample suggestions for parents to help reinforce math at home:

Kindergarten: "Nature Walk"

- Look for dandelions in your yard. Have your child count as many as he/she can. Dig up several and compare the length of their roots. Ask your child which is the longest, which is the shortest.

- Have your child count orally the number of steps needed to get across your yard. Then compare the number of steps taken by him/her with the number of steps needed for other family members. Variations: skipping, jumping, hopping, etc.

- Take a counting walk. Let your child count the trees, shrubs, plants, houses, birds, dogs, or cats, etc. How many of each did he/she see?

- On your walk, see how many numerals you can find. Identify each numeral (on cars, on houses, etc.).

- On your walk, have your child locate and name as many shapes as possible.

First Grade: "Water"

- Give your child a clear glass. Have the child fill the glass until the child thinks it's one-half full. Discuss the answer with your child. Do the same thing with one-fourth.

- Fill a container with water and set it out somewhere in the house. Have your child use a ruler to measure the depth of the water. Write down the numeral on the calendar. At the end of one week, have your child measure the water again. Discuss with your child what happened to the water.

- Help your child follow directions on the sugar-free Kool-Aid packet or frozen juice can to make refreshments for the family.

- Fill glasses that are the same size with different amounts of water. Have your child arrange the glasses from the one that contains the most to the least.

- Take a measuring cup and a quart jar. Have your child guess how many cups it will take to fill the quart container. Use the measuring cup to fill the container and count with your child how many cups it takes to fill the jar.

- Use aluminum foil to make circles, squares, rectangles, and triangles. Fold up sides so the shapes will hold water. Fill, freeze, and have your child look at the shapes and name them.

Second Grade: "Fruits and Vegetables"

- After going to the grocery store, have your child sort fruits and vegetables as you unpack the sack. Sort by canned, fresh and frozen. Items may be counted before putting them away. Variation: Use color or shape.

- Have your child prepare "ants on a log" for a snack for each member of the family. Count one celery stick for each person. Spread peanut butter on each stick (log). Count out five raisins and put on each "log." How many raisins in all?

Third Grade: "Money"

- Give your child a handful of pennies. Hold up a coin and have your child show you the value of the coin in pennies.

- Hold up a coin, have your child identify it and then discuss with him/her what they could buy with it at the store.

- Show your child two or more coins. Have him/her tell you the total value of the coins. Repeat with other sets of coins.

- Write a money value in cents on a sheet of paper. Ask your child to select coins to represent this value (e.g., 23 cents = 2 dimes, 3 pennies).

- When going to the grocery store give your child his/her own money to buy something. Have them select the item to be purchased. They must select something that costs less than the money you have given them. Let them pay for their item(s) at the check-out counter.
  Note: You can use a similar activity when going to McDonald's, Wendy's, or some other fast food restaurant for a meal.

- Give your child a certain amount of imaginary money (e.g., $5.00). Let them use a grocery ad to buy anything they want, staying under the amount of imaginary money given to them.

- Tell your child the price of some item you have purchased (e.g., box of crackers marked 47 cents). Tell them to determine what the fewest number of coins it would take to pay for the item. For the above box of crackers it would be 1 quarter, 2 dimes, and 2 pennies.

Belgrade, Montana, with a population of 3000, buses 60 percent of its 1500 K–12 students. Nonetheless, teachers don't use the wide area their school encompasses as an excuse for not involving parents. K–3 math specialists Terri Goyins and Earlene Hemmer work hard at forging strong community links to their math program. Putting student-made geometric ornaments on display in local businesses is just one way they make school math visible in the community. Goyins and Hemmer send out a math calendar with a daily math problem parents might talk about with their children. These activities show both parents and children the wide range of concerns encompassed by this subject we call mathematics. The Belgrade math calendar for April, "Mathematics Month," includes sports scores, making change, measurement, reading a speedometer, telling time, calendar study, patterns, prediction, spatial relationships, and so on.

A recommended problem such as, "There are four bottles in each case. If I need 36 bottles, how many cases will there be?" demonstrates to parents and children that "doing" mathematics involves active thinking; mathematics is not mere memorization, number shoving, or answer-grabbing. Such a problem demonstrates to parents that mathematics is not a set of facts to be learned but an approach, a vehicle for problem solving. Such a problem shows parents that when educators stress the importance of problem solving, they don't mean just changing the labels on the tired old chestnut numeration problem of the apples and oranges variety. *Math News,* the newsletter for parents in Brywood/Santiago Hills Elementary Schools in Irvine, California, communicates a similar message to parents: "Problem solving is the heart of our instructional program in mathematics. It traditionally means word problems, but it is a process, not a distinct topic. When we talk about problem solving skills, we are talking about ways we learn how to think about a problem. We might look for a pattern, draw a picture, work backwards; we work by choosing the best of many possibilities." Math specialists around the country are quick to point out to parents that the process is what's important; children's efforts need to be applauded; they need to come to know that mathematics is not an either/or situation, one where you find the right answer or you don't. Parents are not hard to convince when they witness their first graders as well as their third graders tackling a problem such as the 36-bottle puzzler on their own—and coming up with creative strategies to figure it out. As one parent put it, "I don't believe the newspaper headlines about declining math skills when I watch my six-year-old inventing a way to divide! She is confident in her ability to solve any type of problem—and so am I!"

Believing that making math visible in the community—to parents as well as their children—helps children see a reason for studying math, Goyins and Hemmer contact local businesses and solicit their help in making real-life mathematics visible. These teachers compiled an extensive directory of community businesses willing to participate—from lumber yards to banks to restaurants. Men and women who come to classrooms and talk about how they use math in their jobs become math role models. Everyone is surprised by how long this mathematics resource list has become—and how pervasive mathematics really is in Belgrade, Montana. And it isn't all talk. Dan Gustafson, manager of the local IGA store, is a popular figure in the school. He has been in every elementary classroom, making pizza with students, as we saw in an earlier chapter. They talk math-in-action as they measure, write directions, think about quantity—and just how many pieces they will get to eat. At the 1991 Math Olympics opening ceremony, Gustafson presented the official problem to each group of students. The effect of having a member of the business community, someone children and their parents see at his place of business several times a week, show such an interest in an active kind of math is powerful—for children and their parents.

Schools in Columbia, Missouri, have forged an alliance with the Engineering Department at a local university. Both university students and practicing engineers come into classrooms and engage students in such topics as the mathematics of bridge building. The professionals talk about bridges, show pictures and models of bridges, and then help students build a few bridges of their own. Linda Solomon, a third grade teacher in Albuquerque, New Mexico, reports that parents ask, "What on earth is happening in math? My children are so happy." Happy and achieving. Solomon notes that at open house parents are stumped on a place value activity—until their children show them how to do it.

Lois Folsom, director of the K–3 Math Specialist Project in Albuquerque, says that in Albuquerque "everybody wrote the project." Very much aware of the failure rate of top-down models, the Albuquerque advisory committee reflects the egalitarian nature of the project itself; it includes three parents, three classroom teachers, and three principals. "It is crucial to bring parents in from the start if you want their support later on," observes Folsom. One parent member of the advisory council also coordinates the Family Math program. A classroom volunteer, she offers strong testimony to the fact that math phobia crosses socioeconomic lines and educational backgrounds. It isn't just uneducated, poverty stricken people who are illiterate in mathematics. "Being involved in the Exxon grant has turned our family's life around. As a nurse, I knew math was important to me, but I'd never been comfortable with math in school or in college, never really understood the math involved in my job. The math had never been made concrete for me. Seeing the way math is done in my children's classrooms, seeing—and understanding—the concrete base, has given me confidence. My husband [a physician] feels the same way. He memorized advanced calculus but never understood it. He feels he missed out on the significance of math because he was too busy memorizing so he could ace the tests." She pauses and smiles. "Our second grader loves math—loves finding unknowns. Can you imagine? Finding unknowns in second grade? But he did it last year too. He's been doing algebra since first grade. And, even better, he understands what he's doing." This parent brought her newfound enthusiasm for mathematics into the "Celebration of Children" school fair, incorporating interactive math posters into the displays. She explains, "The fair used to be just art displays. Now we're putting math on display too, showing how aesthetically pleasing it can be. We're bringing math to a fun level; we're saying 'Hooray for math!'"

A parent in Columbia, Missouri, gives evidence of this same feeling when she writes to the teacher, "Sometimes it's difficult to make math fun, and I'm looking for suggestions. What you're doing is fun. My son talks about it every day. Can you give me ideas to continue this at home?"

Sandra Young's journal reflects both the concerns of parents and their willingness to support new ideas. A second grade teacher and math specialist at Dr. Phillips Elementary School in Orlando, Florida, Young notes early in November during the implementation year of the project that parents who come in for the first conference don't ask why math dittos aren't going home, though they do ask "some really good questions about how I am fitting practice of computation into my math program." Young continues, "Another mother asked me to explain why I did not give the answers to the children during problem-centered learning. After our discussion she did not seem concerned anymore." Significantly, a teacher who has received extensive training in a new curriculum approach appreciates parents' questions and concerns rather than being threatened by them. Young summarizes the parent conferences: "Not one parent told me that their child did not enjoy what was going on in the class. Not one parent said they thought their children weren't learning."

In a later journal entry, Young comments about a Betty Boop game the children play to practice grouping in other bases. "I thought they might get bored with it, but we have had to play it every day this week! I have had two moms call me to ask me to explain what exactly I was doing since their children wanted them to play it at home. The moms didn't understand how Betty Boop would have anything to do with math!"

Pumpkin Empanadas and Other Lessons Outside School

When asked to explain the school's mathematics program to the Tucson League of Women Voters, teacher Chris Confer decides to tell them about Delia Hakim's first grade classroom. Hakim starts every unit of study from the assumption that her students already know a lot because their parents have taught them a lot, directly and indirectly. As contrasted with the unused science text in her classroom that assumes that children are empty vessels waiting to be filled with information, Hakim arranges activities to find out what they already know. In her words, "The children will be scientists; they will be mathematicians. They need to see that mathematics is active, not passive." This often means getting out of the classroom and investigating in the real world. Since Hakim starts from the assumption that parents, too, are knowledgeable, she enlists their aid. "We can profit from their knowledge—instead of assuming they, too, are empty vessels waiting for us to give them our knowledge." Rather than cooking pumpkin empanadas at school, Hakim opts to take her first graders to a parent's house; she leaves the organization of the morning's learning experience in the hands of two mothers who supervise the making of empanadas. While the first graders mix, shape, and cook empanadas, the mothers integrate math, vocabulary, reading, history, and nutrition "skills." Confer and Hakim note that these mothers need neither teacher supervision nor scope and sequence checklists to provide a rich across-the-curriculum, real-world lesson. Confer concludes, "Restructuring schools will require adults to work together in new ways." One of these ways will include welcoming parents and other adults in the community as colleagues with special talents and insights to share.

Chapter

Who's Afraid of Evaluation?

Ask most teachers how students are evaluated in their district, and more often than not they react as if you had just screeched your fingernail down the chalkboard. Evaluation has become a political carrot: standardized tests that children take as often as four or five times a year are used as a way to evaluate teachers and schools, sell real estate, and further the ambitions of politicians. Houses are advertised as being in school districts with above average test scores; secretaries of education point to test score graphs as though they were some sort of Dow Jones average. Lost in this numbers blitz is much concern about how the constant and continual testing in schools affects the day-to-day learning of individual children.

The people who write the tests are also critical of the multifarious ways these test scores are used. Even test writers will admit that standardized tests have a narrow range of valid use and do not necessarily measure what a child knows. Unfortunately, whenever educators try to point out that newspaper listings of schools' standardized achievement test results—ostensibly published as a public service—distort what's happening in schools, they are made to sound like the captain on the Titanic who wants the world to know that the trumpeter who's sinking with him has never played so well. Standardized test scores do provide one small piece of information about a school; too bad so few people stick around for the rest of the story.

Visit good math classrooms across this country and you will see students working with partners, in small teams, and by themselves. You will also see students using a variety of resources: texts, manipulatives, calculators, and computers. As they work on an impressive array of projects over an extended period of time, students know they have a variety of people with whom they can consult: other students, their teachers, various administrators who spend their time in classrooms rather than behind desks, and community helpers. These students are challenged by math concepts that were not mentioned a decade ago; enthusiastic primary graders go home and teach their parents about everything from graphing family members' armspans to constructing tessellations, to turning numbers into art. If you want evidence of math excitement and thoughtfulness, then just take a look at student math journals. Even kindergartners keep personal records of their thinking in math.

The Agony of April

Math class is a wonderful place to be—until spring. Soon after the Ides of March, comes the "Agony of April," when the school's thoughtful, active, child-specific mathematics program gets shoved into a closet—to make room for skill-drill practice for "The Test." Children must get ready to prove they've made "progress" on the kinds of discrete items disconnected from any meaningful context that appear on standardized tests, items than can be scored by a machine. Simple addition, subtraction, multiplication, and division problems are the staples of standardized tests. The hands-on, real-world participatory mathematics that engages children—the kind of learning that helps them capitalize on their strengths while they work on their weaknesses—is replaced by drill and practice for a solitary performance on a timed test that everybody hates. Speed is the first priority on such tests; thoughtfulness is penalized.

Paradoxically, even as the U.S. Department of Education publicizes standardized test results and calls for yet another national test, the U.S. Department of Labor issues a report, *What Work Requires of Schools*, showing that business and industry need "fundamental competencies" quite different from those skills measured by the tests. Among the necessary skills pinpointed in this report are: managing time, working with others, acquiring and using information, understanding complex interrelationships, and working with a variety of technologies.

In addition to these basic skills, the Secretary of Labor's Commission on Achieving Necessary Skills calls for the ability "to make deci-

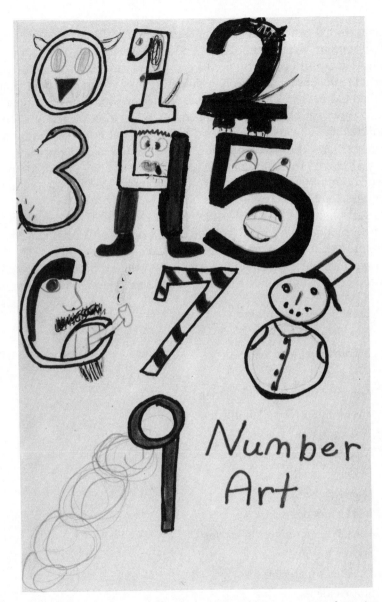

Across the country children are encouraged to see numbers in new ways.

sions and reason clearly, and to assume responsibility, enjoy earned self-esteem, and be ethical."

These are the qualities sneered at by a bullying Secretary of Education operating from a pulpit (and also attacked by religious fundamentalist groups who want nothing smacking of "values" or "personal development" in the schools). But if Washington, D.C., bureaucrats take a short view and if, for them, third grade mathematics is as foreign as particle physics or Petrarchan sonnets, they do understand politics. And so if during hard times Fortune 500 boardrooms turn to consciousness conversation and begin to articulate the importance of such soft qualities as self-esteem and good interpersonal communication skills, then perhaps there is hope for the Department of Education. Who knows? Maybe these bureaucrats, who for years have insisted on standardized number-crunching for the programs it funds, may well have to examine some of its biases.

Although the idea of learning to work with others, manage time, and be responsible for one's actions is a novelty to Washington, D.C., bureaucrats, it is a longstanding value in elementary schools. The Cherry Crest Elementary School in Bellevue, Washington, uses the following list to help them evaluate the progress of their primary level students:

Gets along with others

Practices self-control

Is courteous/kind/helpful

Is punctual

Accepts/fulfills responsibilities

Shows initiative/self-motivated

Willing to risk

Adapts to change

Displays positive attitude

Uses time well

Works independently

Works cooperatively in groups

Strives for quality work

Organizes materials

Shares ideas

The school rating system is: M= Most of the time; P = Part of the time; N = Not yet. The "not yet" is as significant as the "most of the time." Who among us is at his best all of the time? Or at his worst all of the time? With such a marking system, teachers in this school don't put kids in camps of permanent success or failure. Everyone is on a continuum; nobody is perfect, nobody is written off as a dunce.

Teaching to the Test

Although "teaching to the test" is in disrepute, teachers do it out of a sense of survival, and probably no teachers do it more than those special-needs teachers whose program funds are directly controlled by the federal government. The farther away the money source, the greater is the reliance on standardized test scores. There is plenty of research documenting the fact that children in remedial/corrective/special math and reading classes spend a very large percentage of time practicing the sort of discrete, disembodied, decontextualized skills that are on the standardized tests. Remedial classes practice for "The Test" all year long, and spring is the time when regular classes begin to look more and more like remedial classes. Spring is the time when all but the most iconoclastic of teachers are likely to shut their doors and run skill-drill boot camp. We train our students how to fill in the little bubbles with number 2 pencils, and we give them "practice drills" on items that closely resemble those on standardized tests. The truly desperate among us even make a secret purchase of those nasty workbooks that give students lots of drill and practice on test questions. In fact, there is a whole "test preparation series"; schools can buy workbooks to prepare students for the Stanford Achievement Test (SAT), the Comprehensive Tests of Basic Skills (CTBS), the California Achievement Tests (CAT), the Iowa Tests of Basic Skills (ITBS), and the Metropolitan Achievement Tests (MAT). Rather like cigarette and alcoholic beverage warning labels, a disclaimer is listed below each catalogue description: "These books have neither been authorized nor endorsed by [the publisher of the test]." Interestingly, three of these standardized tests are published by Macmillan/McGraw-Hill, which also publishes the test-practice books.

But all this seems insignificant when compared with what has really gone amok with standardized achievement test taking: the "Lake Wobegon effect," in which "all the children are above average." In 1987, when physician John Jacob Cannell announced the results of his study of states' results on nationally normed achievement tests, showing that all fifty states report above-average scores on six major achievement tests—in every subject at every elementary grade level—many academics dismissed Cannell as "unqualified." Then the U.S. Department of Education funded an $80,000 project at the University of California, Los Angeles, to replicate Cannell's study and found that "the overall percent of students above the national median is greater than 50 in all the elementary grades in both reading and mathematics for each of the three years studied."

This is partly a result of using old tests with outdated norms. Test makers don't renorm all that frequently, and many districts administer the same tests for twenty years or more. Districts don't do this just to save money; rather, they know they score better against old norms. Part of this "Lake Wobegon effect" is a result of the political pressure to equate testing with accountability. In this era of "high-stakes testing," schools in such states as Kentucky, Indiana, and South Carolina receive state-funded bonuses based on standardized test scores. And standardized test publishers are just about as vocal against using their tests to measure school or district accountability as are educators. The tests were never intended for this purpose.

Ironically, most educators agree that the tests are useless in terms of the higher level skills that reformers claim they want students to know. Given enough practice, students can indeed get better and better at rudimentary skills; they can all be "above average" on math facts. Once students have taken a particular test eight times or so (and by then they might be only in the third grade), they—and their teachers— are very familiar with that test, and so the result is an above-average school.

In his book *In the Name of Excellence*, Thomas Toch, education correspondent for *U.S. News & World Report*, describes a number of districts in which the superintendent's obsession with standardized test scores has reached loony levels but has brought the district a national reputation for excellence. Where student art once hung in conference rooms, superintendents now hang charts of the CAT scores for every school in the district. They have been using the same version of the CAT for a decade and are very resistant to changing tests. In some districts, for two months before the CAT testing, students receive an extra hour of computer time each day to practice multiple-choice questions; teachers are shown videos on creative ways to prepare students for the CAT; and so on.

Of course, the "Lake Wobegon effect" is somewhat a case of delivering to the public what it has asked for. Surprisingly, the public wants average: not too low, but not too high, either. According to the *Report on Education Research*, 70 percent of the parents questioned said that "they wanted a school with above average or average exam scores." Fewer than a third of the parents said they wanted "a school with very high achievement and accreditation marks"; most feared that such a school might put too much pressure on their children.

Just what do these "above average" results mean? Lauren Resnick and Daniel Resnick argue that American students are the "most tested" but the "least examined" students in the world. Resnick and Resnick point out that our penchant for assessing curriculum components encourages exercises in which isolated components are practiced. "But since the components do not 'add up to' thinking and problem solving, students who practice only the components are unlikely to learn to do real problem solving or interpretive thinking."

David Hawkins maintains that we must stop putting children on a linear scale when we evaluate them and should use instead a multidimensional scale. Hawkins argues that teachers who are skillful at observation can tell us a great deal that is important about a child, things that statistics cannot detect. The qualities and attributes that skilled teachers can perceive and describe, Hawkins insists, are too numerous and varied to catalogue, but they do show an accurate picture of children. Many schools might say that they would like to try evaluating children in this way, but it isn't practical. "Nonsense!" Hawkins scoffs. "In thinking, the only important question is whether it's true or not, not whether it's practical."

Continuing in this vein, Grant Wiggins, a special consultant on assessment and curriculum to both the National Center on Education and the Economy in Rochester, New York, and the Coalition of Essential Schools, notes that we need to figure out what we actually want students to be good at—and leave our concerns about grading their performance on these qualities until later. This sounds very like Hawkins's assertion that truth is more important than practicality. Wiggins believes that we tend to get so caught up in finding a fair, efficient, and objective method of grading students' performance that we forget that this grading is an ancillary problem to the primary concern of content and methodology; in short, test scoring must not continue to determine the curriculum.

Lisa

The decontextualization in standardized tests was brought home when my own third graders took the annual New York State test. The teacher's instruction manual cautioned that I must not offer help in interpreting test questions, so when my students began complaining that there was no right answer for problem 48, I just muttered, "Do your best." Finally, though, I tried to solve problem 48 myself:

A kickball team has just two players on it. How many teams can be made by using Tom, John, and Lisa?
A. 6 C. 3
B. 2 D. 4

No wonder my students were stumped. I couldn't find a right answer, either. On a third grade test! An emergency call to the principal—who prided himself on his command of mathematics—didn't produce an answer. Before long, the whole building was buzzing about problem 48.

Of course, we eventually figured out that the problem called for commutation, substituting or replacing items—in this case items in a pair—but couldn't this have been made clearer? My third graders loved commutative problems, but I interpreted this question just as literally as they did: If you're standing on a field with two other kids, you can't have three teams (the correct answer) simultaneously (well, maybe you can; read on). And if you're eight years old and standing on a field ready to play, who cares about theoretical teams?

My students knew me. "Write a letter!" they urged. And so I did. I grabbed Eddie's test booklet as a reference. Eddie surprised—and pleased—me. He had dutifully filled in an oval on his answer sheet, but he also felt a need to explain himself to the tester. Eddie wrote, "There is one team really. Lisa can't play until someone gives her a turn."

The next day I asked Eddie about his answer. He explained, "Since Lisa was listed last, I figured she got there last. She has to wait her turn." I told Eddie I was glad he hadn't based his decision on some sort of sexist prejudice, glad that he would have left Tom out had he arrived last. For the rest of the year, whenever Eddie's classmates wanted a laugh, they'd chant, "Eddie won't let Lisa play because he doesn't like girls." My students might have missed the question, but Lisa was immortalized. Students soon forgot about Tom and John, but every so often, someone would remember Lisa. When we went on a field trip, the kids asked, "Can Lisa come?" When Brian's mother brought in cupcakes for his birthday, he explained that the extra one was for Lisa.

Unfortunately, the New York State Education Department Mathematics Bureau lacks that third grade sense of whimsy. None of us liked the bureau chief's reply: "Your student who stated that there is only one team and Lisa cannot play forgot that there is also a possible team on which Tom cannot play and a third possible team on which John cannot play. The question asks how many teams can be made up." I wanted to urge the bureau chief to "lighten up." By then, my students knew the "right" answer but were more interested in the alternatives. It had never been my motive to garner more points for my students on the exam. Rather, I had thought the education department functionary just might be charmed by my third graders' attempts to solve the problem in a practical, real-kid way. But he was not charmed by Eddie's reasoning or by the reasoning of other children, for it turned out a number of my students had violated the injunction against writing in the test booklet.

Unwilling to abandon our "write about it" philosophy simply because it was testing day, the children assumed that the New York State Education Department officials would be interested in their reasoning. Most of the students figured out that if the numbers were immovable, the game rules weren't; they invented new rules so that everybody could play. Some suggested that the third person could be the scorekeeper; Sarah thought it would be fun to have three one-person teams on the field simultaneously. The children might not have recognized a commutation problem, but they certainly recognized the need to apply divergent thinking to game rules. Throughout the year I had worked hard at making math touch their lives, and so it simply did not occur to these third graders that somebody would want to know how many different theoretical two-person teams there could be—without actually playing the game.

To his credit, my principal saw the incident as a valuable learning experience. He talked over possible answers with the children, and he also brought in all sorts of interesting number stories. He tried to get our district curriculum coordinator interested, but her reaction was that those fellows at the State Department of Education must know what they're doing. She wondered if we didn't have anything better to do in third grade than argue about a test question.

In *Grammatical Man*, Jeremy Campbell observes that "the brain does not like randomness. If the items in a list have no obvious relationship, no discernible pattern, the brain will invent relationships." My third graders invented a whole culture for Lisa and her teammates. As they discussed and argued over their solutions and moved numbers around, one question in one math test came alive right before our eyes. Because teachers' discontent with standardized tests grows out of a desire and finally a determination to observe and document what students actually do in math class—search for pattern, for relationships, for connections to the world they know—this test, perversely, just might have achieved that.

Just the Facts, Ma'am

Perhaps I dwell too long on one question from one test, especially when the test as a whole was a good one. Of course, the fact that my students liked the test presented even more complications. They could not understand why they weren't allowed to take the test home to show off to their parents what they could do. We shared all their other work. Why did tests have to be locked up in vaults both before and after they were administered? I dwell on this whole episode because I'm bothered when the people in charge won't take third graders seriously, won't see that there might be a message in all this. When Raymond Chandler's Marlowe is asked, "Which side are you on, Marlowe?" he replies, "I don't even know which teams are playing." Too many people who make critical judgments about education in this country have the same problem.

In a more reasonable world, tests would not be locked up. If tests weren't filled with such bilge, teaching to the test would not be a shameful act. If the tests made sense, if they truly reflected the kind of curriculum advocated by such professional organizations as the NCTM (not to mention the Secretary of Labor's Commission on Achieving Necessary Skills), then teaching for the test could only enrich education. But in our current arrangement, the tail wags the dog and teaching to the tests is the last refuge of the scoundrel. We choose our tests for all the wrong reasons: for their ease of administration and their cost effectiveness of scoring. We choose our tests so everybody can be above average.

All the above criticism of standardized tests is understated. Jerrold Zacharias, professor of physics at the Massachusetts Institute of Technology and a leading developer of science materials for young children, said a decade ago, "I feel emotionally toward the testing industry as I would toward any other merchant of death. I'm not saying that they murder every child—only 20 percent of them." More than two decades ago the late Banesh Hoffman, a prominent scientist and educator, carefully documented the insanity of standardized tests, pointing out that "multiple-choice tests are inherently defective no matter how well they are drafted." Hoffman was also concerned with what all this standardized measuring does to these children. As soon as you complain that multiple-choice tests narrow the curriculum by encouraging teachers to focus on "just the facts," on basic skills, then both the knee-jerk back-to-the-basics hardheads and the jelly-limbed anything-that-makes-you-happy softheads misconstrue this to be advocacy for ignoring basic number facts. Nobody with any common sense wants eighteen-year-olds to take their multiplication facts charts off to college or thirty-six-year-olds to count on their fingers every time they subtract double digits, and no one but a paranoid pessimist believes this will happen. The point is not *if* children are going to learn these things, but *when*.

For the seemingly simple memorization chores—number facts, spelling demons, and the apostrophe—timing is everything. One of the things that makes teaching a specialized craft involving art, science, intuition, empathy, discipline, creativity, and a healthy sense of humor is the teacher's combination of sensibility and sensitivity, her ability to figure out when, for the individual student, the time is right to say, "O.K., tonight I'd like you to practice your sixes." What drives the hardheads crazy is that a sensible and sensitive teacher probably won't say this to most third graders. Rather, she is willing to give children time to form their own firm foundations of mathematical understanding before she imposes memorization of a specific algorithm. Too often we get so caught up in arguments about these pesky basic facts that we forget that they are truly the red herring, distracting attention from more important matters.

The real irony is that those people advocating assessment reform are striving for more rigor in the curriculum, not less. People who support performance-based assessment are not saying that once we give children calculators and computers they don't need to know how to add and subtract or memorize the times tables. Rather, they are saying that such operations, once the sole content of elementary arithmetic study, are not nearly enough for the mathematics-impacted world of the twenty-first century. What proponents of performance-based assessment insist is that improved tests will raise curriculum standards, that the schools will then expect their students to do more, not less. Ramsay W. Seldon, director of the education assessment center for the Council of Chief State School Officers, points to the curriculum message that accompanies the new tests: "Teachers still have to be shown how to teach in new ways. That has to be accomplished by professional development and reeducation of teachers." The Bellevue, Washington, public schools inject the reeducation of parents and administrators as well as teachers into the equation, so that traditional outsiders become privy to insider information about how schools work.

One District's Mission

This link between new student assessment methods and educator-parent study teams convinced me to go to Bellevue. When Sherry Beard, elementary mathematics specialist for the Bellevue public schools, talked about her district's ten-year effort to improve math education, she stressed the need to give teachers the opportunity to clarify and articulate what they value—and to do this jointly with administrators and parents. I knew I wanted to hear more.

Bellevue's position on standardized testing can be found in a document it published in 1988 entitled *Elementary Study*. It lists standardized tests as one of fourteen ways of assessing students' performance. Regarding standardized tests as just one resource among a multitude is not a "me too" position for Bellevue, not a case of its trying to jump on the latest educational bandwagon. This suburban Seattle district's mathematics reform program is ongoing; there is no culminating document. The impressively long and provocative paper trail leading to Bellevue's position on standardized testing—and beyond—suggests that a culminating document, a final report, would be contrary to their basic beliefs. This is a district committed to staff development coupled with parent involvement on an intellectual as well as a practical level, a district that supports change over time. Beard notes that university people like to work with Bellevue schools because "we're in things for the long haul. We follow through on the long-term aspects of change."

At the core of Bellevue's commitment is its adherence to school-centered decision making and its recognition of parents as respected and necessary partners in school change. For a number of districts throughout the United States these terms became *pro forma* buzzwords in the mid-1980s, but Bellevue's approach quickly cuts through rhetoric. Parents join the same study teams and attend the same training sessions as do administrators and teachers. Most study teams have five members: a parent, three teachers (chosen by the school staff), and the principal. In 1990, Beard approached the Exxon Education Foundation with a research proposal on behalf of the school district. The Foundation agreed to support an assessment project study team, bringing together the school study teams for monthly meetings and providing this central team of more than eighty people with the necessary resources for a year of learning about assessment. In that year they produced the following *Mission Statement for K-5 Mathematics Assessment*:

> The Bellevue School District is committed to K–5 Mathematics assessment which provides for a continuous, authentic, equitable process of assessing children using a variety of developmentally appropriate tools. The purposes of such assessment are to refine instruction*; to involve the child in the evaluation process*; and to inform teachers, parents, and community members of children's mathematical understanding*.

* *To refine instruction, assessment should:*

> Be aligned with the K–5 Mathematics Student Learning Objectives (SLOs):
>
> Involve complex items that address more than one SLO, thereby representing the complexity of mathematics in the world;
>
> Be a dynamic process, thereby subject to review and change;
>
> Provide challenge and engage all children;
>
> Be done individually and in groups;

Provide opportunities for success to all children; and,

Recognize and value a range of learning styles.

* To involve the child in the evaluation process, assessment should:

Provide a format where the child is expected to explain his/her thinking process in a variety of ways (written, oral, using materials, etc.);

Engage the child in problems he/she hasn't yet seen;

Have the child use mathematical processes, such as computation, in the context of problems rather than in isolation;

Present opportunities where the child uses mathematics to make sense of complex situations;

Provide the child with access to the same types of materials used in the classroom, i.e., manipulatives, calculators, computers;

Not use time as a factor, since speed is almost never relevant in mathematical effectiveness;

Enhance the child's motivation and commitment to learning; and

Promote the child's ability to assess his/her own understanding.

* To inform teachers, parents, and community members, assessment should:

Demonstrate how the child's understanding develops over time;

Define and communicate standards to teachers, students, parents, and the community;

Be reported in a clear and meaningful way;

Focus on what the child knows, rather than on what he/she does not know; and,

Provide useful, and easily accessible, information to the teacher for refining instruction.

Beard talks of the "miracle" of getting more than eighty people to bring their ideas together in such a document. With exploration and a mission statement in the first year, the study team focused the second year on "action research," developing sample assessments; a third year will include piloting assessment models.

When consultants such as Kathy Richardson or Mary Lindquist or Judy Mumma or Marilyn Burns or Jan Mokros are brought in to lead workshops about alternative assessment, parents attend right along with teachers and administrators, thus learning about issues firsthand. Parents become acquainted right along with the teachers with new evaluation strategies such as portfolio assessment. When parents work with teachers to come up with alternative assessments, rather than becoming antagonists facing an incomprehensible fait accompli at Back to School Night, as happens in so many districts, they understand the issues involved and are able to communicate the reasons for the change to other parents. In the words of Bellevue Superintendent Don O'Neil, "Parents are our strongest advocates, our best spokespeople in the community."

I saw proof of parent advocacy when I heard one parent remind another who was complaining about her child's not having a Friday spelling test, "A teacher needs to test what she values, and that teacher values writing fluency more than spelling. I wish I'd had such a teacher: I'm a terrible speller and always felt I was a terrible writer because of that."

After members of the assessment project study team attend a workshop, Beard sends a memo summarizing the reactions, pointing out that the purpose of the workshop is not to be "sold" on a particular approach, such as portfolio assessment. She keeps reminding both parents and teachers, "We aren't here to make decisions; we're here to learn. We don't need to make a choice yet; in fact, we shouldn't make a choice yet." She repeats, "We need to learn." Beard helps the assessment project study team keep focused on the fact that:

> You get what you assess;
>
> You don't get what you don't assess;
>
> You have to build assessments that you want people to teach to.

Administrators, teachers, and parents on the study team are given suggestions for sharing information with the larger school community—everything from sharing rubric scoring with colleagues to publishing articles in the PTA newsletter. Don O'Neil holds quarterly coffee meetings, inviting the community to attend and voice their concerns. O'Neil maintains that often the perception of math in the larger community is: "Tell the kid this is math. That's it. Kids who do what they're told grow up to be scientists." He adds that informed parents are the best weapon against such simplicities.

Where Are the Report Cards?

I get a big laugh when I ask whether I might see a report card, and I am informed that there is no single elementary report card in Bellevue. As one mother points out, "My children attend the same school, and they have different report cards." A teacher admits, "I've changed my report card format every year; one year I changed it twice." Report card formats in the district range from a piece of paper containing nothing but the school letterhead (leaving lots of room for the teacher's comments about the child's strengths and weaknesses) to a fourteen-page form with goals on one side and a checklist on the other. The latter is famous in the district. "You haven't heard about our report card?" a teacher smiles at me in mock surprise, explaining that the form has become a way of helping staff and parents understand the developmental nature of learning. "Parents come in expecting us to say, 'This is what Johnny can do, and this is what he needs to do.' Instead, we say, 'This is where Johnny is.' "

None of the elementary schools gives letter or number grades. Teachers and administrators proudly tell me that elementary schools in Bellevue haven't given grades for thirty years. But I soon learn that this does not happen without an ongoing sense of ambivalence and very real frustration. Teachers as well as parents keep reminding themselves: "We don't want grades; we don't want grades." One primary grade teacher explains that she sends home a list of student learning objectives every time they start a new topic. "I know this informs parents much more than grades ever could. It's a lot more work, but it's worth it."

A parent tells me, "I go to these meetings and learn new methods for doing things, and I think it's all wonderful; I admire these teachers for all the work they put into trying to treat each child as an individual. But then I get home and I still wonder, 'Is my child doing all right?' A percentage score can be reassuring. I get different report cards from different teachers. I admit that there's a part of me that would like to know, in a group of twenty-five kids, how my child is doing."

A teacher counters, "At work, does a manager rate an employee and tell him how he's doing in percentages when measured up to other employees?" She adds, "I teach a mixed grade class. When parents insist on knowing whether their child is doing second grade or third grade work, I ask them whether employees are judged by whether they've they've been on the job one year or five."

Another parent comments, "On the one hand, I kind of wish for grades, but on the other hand, I love the fact that my child is rated on an individual basis. I know I wish I had been taught this way. I remember those time tests and getting sweaty palms; I was so anxious. It was horrible. Now kids are playing games in math, and I want to play, too."

Still another parent agrees. "My son is not a good test taker, and so I appreciate the fact that his teachers look for different ways of assessing his strengths—and his weaknesses." She smiles and adds, "Actually, my son thinks he's wonderful in math."

A teacher says that she finds students are quite realistic about their talents. "A little before conference time, I invite my students to complete open-ended statements such as 'I believe I can . . . '; 'My teacher thinks...'; 'I think I need . . .' Students are amazingly accurate about where they are strong and what they need to work on."

A parent admits, "I'm wrestling with form versus creativity. My son's penmanship is so terrible. So the teacher suggests teaching him typing. Another teacher says, 'Maybe he'll be a doctor.' I appreciate the options, I guess, but don't children need to be taught some formalistic structure? The teachers assure us 'That will come.' I admit I'm frustrated—not quite disagreeing—just bothered."

Another parent offers, "Change is very uncomfortable—for parents as well as teachers. I think we're scared we might lose something and we don't want our children to be . . ." She pauses, and everyone else around the table inserts, "guinea pigs." Everybody laughs.

"I agree. I'm worried that we're throwing out standardized tests. I want to know where my child is in relation to other students in this state and the nation.

"I'll tell you, I want to know where my child is in relationship to the children in Japan. That scares me. We're constantly hearing comparisons of our country with other countries, and it's frightening. And because I'm frightened, I try to fill in what I think my son is not getting in school. I know my son is receiving logic, geometry, and all that in school, so I give him computation at home."

Another parent joins in. "Marilyn Burns spoke to that in her workshop. She sees her role as a teacher as being one to inspire the child to go home and memorize those facts because it is more efficient to know the facts than not." Other parents grin, and one adds, "It does take a lower level skill to help a child memorize the math facts; we should leave the higher skills to the teachers."

Making Parents Feel Better

Although I am attending this meeting as an observer, I can't resist mentioning an article I'd read on the plane that runs counter to the doom-and-gloom media reports about schools. National Education Association research psychologist and policy analyst Gerald W. Bracey offers a persuasive argument that things are better than they ever were in the United States education system ("Why Can't They Be Like We

Were?" *Phi Delta Kappan*, October 1991). Bracey demonstrates convincingly that the "Schools stink!" message we've been hearing so loudly and so constantly for the past decade is not true. Moreover, insists Bracey, *"American schools have never achieved more than they currently achieve"* [emphasis his]. Among other examples Bracey provides is the fact that parents who found calculus to be an arcane and impossible subject, one not encountered—if ever—until college, now have children who routinely study calculus in high school. The media informs us that employers can't find skilled workers, but Bracey points out that more students than ever are graduating from high school, and they're doing better on standardized tests. Although employers do express concern about the "skills" of young workers, they are worried about such qualities as work ethic and social skills such as interpersonal communication. Fully 65 percent of training dollars in business are not spent to increase the basic skills of unskilled or skilled laborers but to augment the skills of college graduates.

Bracey points out that the schools are hardly responsible "for the management decisions that kept Detroit turning out self-destructing, two-ton gas guzzlers until it lost its dominance of the market"; nor did the school's "sloppy pedagogy prevent industry from automating." It is in no way obvious that the decline in our economic standing stems from problems in the schoolhouse—or that these woes will be reversed merely by improving the schools.

You could have cut the parents' relief with a knife. It is clear that these parents are satisfied with the education their children are receiving; they would just like a voice with the definitiveness of *Newsweek* or Dan Rather to agree with them. Educational woes for these parents are global issues, not personal concerns.

Our discussion concludes with a parent's observation that she is relieved that this district doesn't "go in for instantaneous projects." She points out, "This one is scheduled to take three years. Who knows? Maybe it will go on for ten years. I am comforted by the fact that people will take the time they need."

Intuition Versus Grade Point Average

Bellevue teachers express the same apprehensions as parents. Even though they are able to articulate the belief that assessment is something that goes on all day long and this continuous assessment leads to instruction, they need to keep reminding themselves; they need to be bolstered in their own expertise. "The whole thing is overwhelming," admits a teacher of a fourth and fifth grade combination class. "There's a part of me that likes the 'cleanness' of percentages. Sometimes when I have to face the parents I wish I had the safety net provided by those percentages. Parents see my room and they are thrilled by all the projects. They say, 'Is this ever neat!' But sometimes there doesn't seem to be enough solid matter to grab on to. I mean, I can't tell them Johnny is a 93 percent. That has a nice definitive ring to it, doesn't it? Never mind Johnny; it makes me sound so precise, so scientific. But instead, I can show Johnny's work; I can describe a lot of his attitudes . . . but as we try to do this for twenty-five students I worry that we are falling into the old trap of jargon. I want to get away from developing a sort of jargon that just substitutes a verbal label for a numeric one."

A colleague laughs and adds, "Anybody who could publish a list of twenty-five different ways to say 'works well with others' or 'is self-motivated' could make a fortune."

Another teacher agrees. "No matter what we report about a child, no matter how detailed is our evaluation, how filled with specific examples and anecdotes, in the end parents still ask, 'How does he compare with other children? Is he average?' We need to develop a new terminology. Parents say they like cooperative learning, but they still want to know how their child rates when compared with other children."

"Right. At least we used to be able to say how Johnny does on times tables. Now I can honestly say, 'I don't know.' But I worry about replacing the specific information of a 93 percent with a teacher's intuition. Most of what we do is, after all, intuition. But I'm afraid that my intuition doesn't have a whole lot of validity with parents. Sometimes it doesn't have a whole lot of validity with me. If we ever dug a bit below the surface politeness, I think we'd find out that parents really would like to know about those times tables. They'd really like a percentage."

"Yes, but all the traditional assessment assumptions of the old bell-shaped curve have been exploded. That really is no more 'objective' than what we're calling teacher intuition. Now we recognize—and demand—that assessment should give us information beyond a raw percentile score. This is hard for parents; god knows, it's hard for us too. But what we're nervously calling intuition is a teacher who works six hours a day with the child. Maybe we need to stop being apologetic about our 'subjectivism' and start realizing that this is pretty well informed intuition." Another teacher jumps in, "Isn't this where the portfolio is helpful? You can sit with parents and show them, 'Yes, Johnny got this piece but here is a piece where he is missing x-component.' We work in a conservative community with parents who were very successful in the old system, parents who want to know 'Is it right or is it wrong?' But they are beginning to accept this new lingo."

"Yes," agrees a fourth and fifth grade teacher, "but it took me all day to 'evaluate' five children . . . and I thought that was pretty good. But what would I do if I didn't have a student teacher in the room?" Nobody responds.

A primary grade teacher offers, "I agree that parents resist change at first, but they do come around. Parents love hands-on mathematics now. They no longer ask for workbooks. We take that for granted now, but I remember their reaction when we first took workbooks away. We sometimes forget that this dramatic conversion took time; we sometimes forget how far we have come, have far the parents have come with us."

Others agree. "Parents are beginning to see math as doing. They're getting used to seeing homework that asks kids to "Count how many doors are in your house" instead of a ditto sheet on addition facts. Especially when we follow up the homework by sending home the kids' graphs of doors."

A teacher laughs. "One of my students read that an albatross has a span of eleven feet. That got us to thinking. We measured everybody's armspan and then the children went home with the assignment to measure the spans of their parents and siblings. They brought the data back and graphed it." Everyone agrees that "albatross homework" has a nice ring to it.

"Parents aren't the only ones who resist change," admits a teacher. "In 1980 I went to math advisory to fight for the Scott Foresman workbook . . . . And then, not only did we not keep the workbook, we ended up throwing out all the textbooks, too. And it wasn't easy for me. I'd move forward a bit; then I'd run back to what I was comfortable with. It was painful and it was difficult." She laughs. "Let's face it: it is still painful and difficult."

Asking Parents to Report on Report Cards

A study conducted by Jan DeLacy reveals that Bellevue parents are less tied to percentages than teachers fear. When asked to respond to an item about their school's reporting procedures (in *The Bellevue Evaluation Study: Studying the Effects of School Renewal*, December 1990, Jan DeLacy, Institute for Study of Educational Policy, University of Washington), parents' replies are provocative. The statement "I am satisfied with the type of information I receive through parent conferences, report cards, etc., concerning my child's performance at his/her school," elicited this response from elementary school parents:

strongly agree	42.0%
agree more than disagree	37.4%
disagree more than agree	15.1%
strongly disagree	5.0%
don't know	0.0%

Here's how secondary parents responded to the same prompt:

strongly agree	14.7%
agree more than disagree	39.7%
disagree more than agree	29.4%
strongly disagree	13.2%
don't know	1.5%

It is provocative to note that all high schoolers receive letter grades on their report cards. Clearly, the parents of high schoolers aren't nearly so satisfied with the information these grades provide as are the parents of elementary students with the absence of such grades. The specificity of letter grades isn't the safety net some elementary teachers long for. They should remind themselves that politicians would think they'd died and gone to heaven if they ever achieved an 80 percent approval rating.

The Principals' Principles

Bellevue principals praise their teachers while recognizing their nervousness about their students being possible guinea pigs in the new assessment procedures. Principals speak to the need for parent education: "When parents read about how far 'behind' the United States is in math and science and then see 'strange' homework, they get nervous." Principals see the parents on the assessment project study team as their greatest asset: "When they understand what's behind these changes, they explain it to other parents." Principals point out that Back to School Night with educators presenting the program is O.K., but Back to School Night with parents presenting the program in the community is much stronger. "Parents are sometimes suspicious of teachers and administrators who just might have an ax to grind; they believe other parents because their own kids' lives are on the line."

Principals point out how powerful in-service participation has been for parents. "We have to remember we're not dealing just with math but with the whole dynamics of change. As we listen to a parent screaming because his child hasn't learned his multiplication facts, we also find out that this parent wasn't very happy about his own math experience. We hear anger, and we try to listen without getting defensive . . . and the parent finally admits, 'Gee, I wish I'd had this kind of math.' We need to let them talk; we need to listen carefully—before we become too defensive. We have to listen to parents as earnestly as we try to reeducate them." He pauses and then adds, "Sometimes they're right." Everybody laughs.

Another principal points out, "Our greatest strength is the past experience of our staff. We aren't dealing with a novice staff. Our staff has built the trust of parents over the years. Parents know these teachers and they have faith in their doing a good job."

I comment that I'm impressed with the obvious mutual admiration and support among central office staff, principals, teachers, and parents as well as their ability to set common goals. The principals agree. "We struggle in this district with restructuring issues; we don't struggle with philosophy. We are cohesive on what we think is good for kids. We are struggling to find enough dollars for manipulatives, for example, so there's a struggle to apportion monies to each school. But we aren't struggling over the fact that manipulatives are important."

Nancy Loorem, supervisor of elementary principals, believes that people interested in staff development must concern themselves with crucial ethical issues. "The way to make real change is to empower teachers to become thinking and reflective practitioners." She insists, "You don't support a teacher or a principal by challenging or threatening her with, 'Everyone is doing this.' Instead, you say, 'Here's some evidence; what do you think about it?'

"If you don't understand the philosophical underpinnings for change and support those underpinnings," Loorem adds, "then you'll just move from Ginn to Houghton Mifflin."

I ask the principals how they keep themselves informed on something like new standards in mathematics. They point to the seven workshops (so far) conducted by national experts for the assessment project study team. Many of them have taken Marilyn Burns's Math Solutions courses and other training in the summer. The consensus is that "nobody has to do it all; we have lots of resources to help us."

"The teacher math leader in our building helps me. I rely on her for articles and other information."

"Sherry [Beard] sends us a lot of articles; she is willing to come out and work with us. We can rely on her to get what the staff and students need."

"Because we try not to be competitive and it's O.K. to be at different stages of knowledge, we are encouraged to concentrate on our strengths. We are realistic about our teachers being stronger in one area than another; in fact, we celebrate this. We have a whole language leader, a technology leader, and a math leader. Nobody has to do it all—including the principal. We are not threatened by the idea of asking for help."

My report card question to the teachers had elicited laughter; I ask a question of the principals that provoked silence: "Do you encounter any immovable objects?"

After a long silence, one principal offers the upbeat view: "Nothing is immovable."

"Well, there's always the state test," points out his colleague. As is typical of tests that move into schools from somewhere else, parts of the test do not relate to the Bellevue mathematics curriculum, and district personnel feel constrained to translate the results to parents. "We aren't getting rid of standardized tests, but we aren't scrapping our curriculum either. So we try to explain the limited usefulness of these tests. We hold on to things that are familiar but then we explain the rest of what we're doing, how far we're going beyond these tests."

This is a district that seems to exemplify an academic golden rule. Administrators seem as protective of their staffs as the staffs are of their students. Principals express concern about supporting risk-taking in their staff, at the same time supporting those teachers who might be coming along more slowly than their colleagues. "We don't want parents comparing one classroom with another; we want the community to realize that even though differences exist, all children are getting a good education."

"But we don't want staff to stagnate either. We have to say to people, 'Are you growing in this area? What can I do to support you?'"

One principal speaks to this feeling of community. "I feel supported throughout this district. I never feel I am hanging out there by myself. Oh, once in a while I may feel it for half an hour, but I know I have all these resources just a phone call away."

I come away from this visit with the educators and parents of Bellevue, Washington, having seen a district that accepts that change takes a long time, a thoughtful district not interested in moving from one fad to another. It is a district where educators and parents are able to laugh at themselves. When I comment to the administrators that "I come from a district that has no goals," they all chuckle and then say, "We have plenty. How many do you want?"

These administrators describe theirs as an "inquiring district, willing to look at itself." As one administrator said, "Historically, we have been willing to use data to make changes. Change is part of the culture of this district; change is something we believe about ourselves." I agree.

Conclusion: Mathematicians for the Twenty-first Century

In keeping with the spirit that sustains and strengthens K–3 Math Projects across the country, it seems only fitting that the children have the last word. These projects are, after all, about children and how we can nurture their mathematical potential.

In Piedmont, California, Nancy Litton's combined class of first and second graders published their own mathematical riddle book. Their favorite riddles have to do with multiples and exhibit their thinking about multiplication (not standard fare for first graders). Nobody is telling these children to memorize $2 \times 4 = 8$; they are enjoying figuring it out on their own—and challenging their classmates with this problem:

What has 8 legs, 2 tails, 4 eyes, and 1 mane?
A lion and a lioness.

In Piedmont, California, a first grader illustrates the math riddle she has written: What has 20 legs, 10 ears, and lives in a barn?

Litton reports that this kind of riddle is a favorite among the class. They don't memorize times tables but they love coming up with ways of challenging each other to think in terms of multiples:

> What has 20 legs, 10 ears, and lives in a barn?
> A pig and her 4 piglets.

Jordan's riddle adds a twist on this theme. He shows that he understands the concept—and is clever enough to turn it on its head, literally:

> What has 6 legs, 10 heads, and 2 wings???
> I don't know but one is sitting on your head.

Max's riddle uses multiples to put a new spin on the theme:

> What has 2 heads, 4 arms, and no legs?
> Two ghosts spinning in the air.

As I visited primary grade classrooms across the country, a glance at the student graphs on the walls showed me in which month most children were born, how many teeth they had lost, what color eyes they have, what type of shoe they were wearing on a given day, the types of pets they'd like to have, their favorite flavor of ice cream, and what vegetables they like. Quite literally, everything from soup to nuts is fair game for data collection and analysis by young mathematicians.

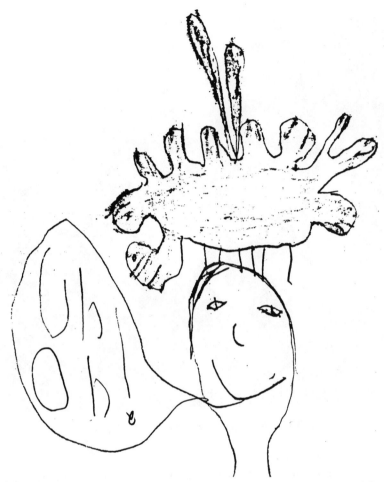

Jordan's illustration answers his riddle: What has 6 legs, 10 heads, and 2 wings?

From kindergartners in Baton Rouge and Orlando to first graders in Las Cruces to third graders in Temecula and Tucson, children think data analysis is great. They are learning to collect data, to transform it into a visual display, to search for hidden patterns. And children don't make graphs just because the teacher tells them to. In Cincinnati, Ohio, Fran Cohen reports that Peter, a six-year-old officially labeled as learning disabled, was so intrigued by graphs that he started collecting lots of data. On his own, Peter kept track of what beverage his classmates chose for snack each day: milk, chocolate milk, or orange juice. He then devised his own system of graphing and reported the results to the class.

Max's riddle asks: What has 2 heads, 4 arms, and no legs?

Children have a way of exceeding textbook expectations when we give them the opportunity. Division isn't introduced until third grade, but don't tell that to first graders in Muncie, Indiana, where teacher Fran Johnson posed this problem:

Twenty-eight children want to go on a field trip. Four children can ride in each car. How many cars do we need?

Andrew writes that 4 children need 1 car, 8 children need 2 cars, and so on. Amir draws 1 car and 4 children and then is unsure of what to do next. Kristi and Adam report on how they solved the problem with Unifix cubes. Tara and Kylemi draw the results of their problem solving using the cubes. Their methods are shown on pages 233–235.

We can rejoice in these first graders' awareness that they are capable of figuring out many ways to solve a problem that is far beyond what

Amir

48 12 16 20 24 28
1 2 3 4 5 6 7

Andrew

Andrew and Amir's car problem.

233

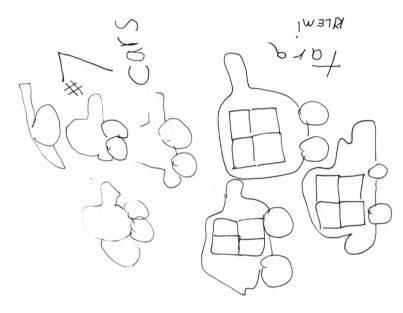

Tara and Kylemi's car problem.

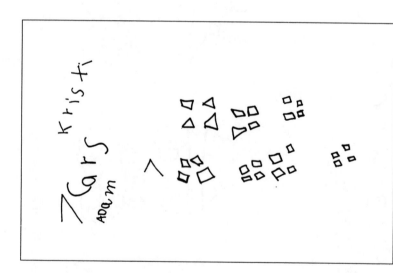

Kristi and Adam's car problem.

The awnser is 15.

Amanda

5-23-90

I got my fingers and counted from 1984 - 1990 and I got 6 so 6+9 = 15

Ramona but she was 9 forever.

In Tampa, Florida, a first grader explains how she solved the Ramona problem—and why she finds the problem inadequate.

the textbooks expect. Such children are excited to communicate their own understanding; they are excited to share their different strategies and learn from their classmates.

In Tampa, Florida, first graders answer the question: "How old would Ramona be today?"

Like children around the country, children in Tampa don't think it's strange that their teacher would ask them a math question about a popular fictional character. They know that the world is filled with mathematics. Amanda checks the copyright date on the popular Beverly Cleary novel and counts up to the current year. She adds that figure to nine, Ramona's age in the story, and gets the "right" answer. But Amanda also knows that getting a number isn't enough, that she must explain her reasoning; Amanda knows she must be able to communicate her mathematical understanding to others in a way that will convince them her answer is correct. So she explains how she got the answer. But even that doesn't satisfy Amanda. Exhibiting the spirit of independent thinking that K–3 Math Project teachers applaud, Amanda takes her mathematics seriously enough to question the premise of the problem. In effect, she says, "Hey, listen up, teachers: I can give you a number, and I can even be confident that number is right, but I also know that Ramona is going to be nine forever."

May 15, 1991

Dear Exxon Corporation,

The best Math project was fiboncci numbers. I got realy into it cause I got to the number 144, It got big! I'll do a good and colorful one fore who evvr is reading this.

Sicerly,
Riley D.

In Belgrade, Montana, students explore Fibonacci numbers.

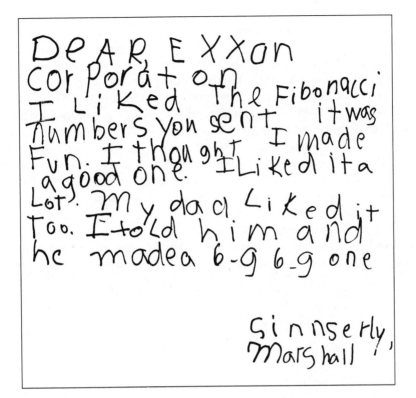

DeAR, EXXon
corporaton
I Liked The Fibonacci
numbers you sent it was
Fun. I thought I made
a good one. I Liked it a
Lot. My dad Liked it
Too. I told him and
he madea 6-9 6-9 one

Sinnserly,
Marshall

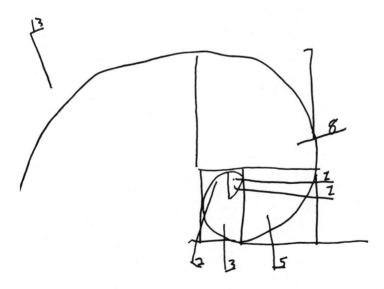

Marshall's letter to Exxon about Fibonacci numbers (sketched from original art).

Marshall and Riley, members of their school's math club in Belgrade, Montana, know that mathematics is full of surprises and wonder and beauty. Chances are, Marshall's dad didn't know mathematics could be beautiful—until Marshall showed off his Fibonacci numbers.

As I look at the work I have collected from thousands of young children across the country, I feel good about these problem solvers for the twenty-first century: children who can think mathematically, who can communicate that thinking to others, who can use mathematics to help them make sense of their lives, who are eager to explore math topics that most of us adults have never heard of. These are children who see themselves as mathematicians, who see math as an integral part of their lives, who are developing a flexible repertoire of problem-solving strategies and attitudes of independent thinking, children who welcome challenge. They know that mathematics can be beautiful. These children are showing us that there is cause for celebration.

The Exxon Education Foundation: K–3 Mathematics Specialist Project Participants

ALABAMA
Butler County School System*
Conecuh County School System*
Huntsville City Schools*

ARIZONA
Tucson Unified School District*

CALIFORNIA
Panama–Buena Vista Union School
  District
Piedmont Unified School District*
San Francisco Unified School District
Temecula Valley Unified School District*
Twain Harte–Long Barn Union
  School District
Ventura Unified School District
Irvine Unified School District*

COLORADO
Jefferson County Public Schools

FLORIDA
Hillsborough County Public Schools*
Orange County Public Schools*
School Board of Volusia County

ILLINOIS
Massac County Unit #1 School District
School District 169, Ford Heights*

INDIANA
Burris–Ball State School Corporation*

IOWA
Iowa City Community School District
Curriculum Consortium of North
  Central Iowa

KANSAS
Wichita Public Schools*

KENTUCKY
Jackson County Public Schools*
Laurel County Board of Education*
Perry County School System
Pulaski County Public Schools

LOUISIANA
Baton Rouge Parish School System*

MAINE
Maine Center for Education

MASSACHUSETTS
Berkshire Hills Regional School District
Worcester Public Schools
Learning Center for Deaf Children*

MINNESOTA
Minnetonka Public School District
  #276

_____

* Classroom profiled in book

239

MISSOURI
Columbia Public Schools*

MONTANA
Alberton Joint District #2
Belgrade School District #44*
Bonner Elementary School District #14
Lolo School District #7

NEW HAMPSHIRE
Portsmouth School District

NEW JERSEY
Montclair State College (with Broadway Elementary School in Newark)

NEW MEXICO
Albuquerque Public Schools*
Bernalillo Public Schools*
Las Cruces School District #2*
Las Lunas Public Schools*

NEW YORK
Brighton Central Schools
Buffalo Public School District
City School District of New Rochelle
City University of New York (for work with six New York City school districts)
Connetquot Central School District of Islip
Ithaca City School District

OHIO
Springer School*

PENNSYLVANIA
Penn Manor School District

RHODE ISLAND
Cranston Public Schools
Narragansett School District

TEXAS
Arlington Independent School District
Friendswood Independent School District
Irving Independent School District
Laredo Independent School District
Trinity University (with two San Antonio elementary schools)
University of Texas, El Paso (with five area school districts)

VIRGINIA
Hanover County Public Schools
Virginia Beach Public Schools

WASHINGTON
Bellevue Public School District*

WEST VIRGINIA
Kanawha County Schools

WISCONSIN
Madison Metropolitan School District
Milwaukee Public Schools*

Further Reading

Armstrong, Thomas. *Awakening Your Child's Natural Genius*. Jeremy P. Tarcher, 1991.

Baker, Ann, and Johnny Baker. *Maths in the Mind*. Heinemann, 1991.

———. *Mathematics in Progress*. Heinemann, 1990.

Baker, Dave, Cheryl Semple, and Tony Stead. *How Big Is the Moon?* Heinemann, 1990.

Baratta-Lorton, Mary. *Mathematics Their Way*. Addison-Wesley, 1976.

Barth, Roland. *Improving Schools from Within: Teachers, Parents, and Principals Can Make the Difference*. Jossey-Bass, 1990.

Bell, E. T. *Men of Mathematics*. Simon & Schuster, 1937.

Brockman, John, ed. *Doing Science: The Reality Club 2*. Prentice Hall, 1991.

———, ed. *Ways of Knowing: The Reality Club 3*. Prentice Hall, 1991.

Brown, Rexford. *Schools of Thought*. Jossey-Bass, 1991.

Bruner, Jerome. *Actual Mind, Possible Worlds*. Harvard University Press, 1986.

Burk, Donna, Allyn Snider, and Paula Symonds. *Box It or Bag It Mathematics*. Math Learning Center, 1988.

Burns, Marilyn. *A Collection of Math Lessons, Grades 3–6*. Math Solutions Publications/Cuisenaire, 1987.

———. *The Good Time Math Event Book*. Creative Publications, 1977.

———. *The I Hate Mathematics! Book*. Little, Brown, 1975.

———. *Math by All Means: Multiplication Grade 3*. Math Solutions Publications/Cuisenaire, 1991.

———. *Math for Smarty Pants*. Little, Brown, 1982.

———. *Mathematics with Manipulatives*. Six videos and teacher discussion guides. Cuisenaire, 1988.

———. *This Book Is about Time*. Little, Brown, 1978.

———, and Bonnie Tank. *A Collection of Math Lessons, Grades 1–3*. Math Solutions Publications/Cuisenaire, 1988.

Buxton, Laurie. *Math Panic*. Heinemann, 1991.

California State Department of Education. *The Changing Mathematics Curriculum: A Booklet for Parents*. California State Department of Education, 1989.

———. *Mathematics: Model Curriculum Guide, K–8*. California State Department of Education, 1989.

Cooney, Thomas J., and Christian R. Hirsch, eds. *Teaching and Learning Mathematics in the 1990s*. NCTM, 1990.

Dale Seymour Publications. *Tessellation Winners: The First Contest*. Dale Seymour, 1991.

Davis, Phillip, and Reuben Hersh. *Descartes' Dream*. Harcourt Brace Jovanovich, 1986.

———. *The Mathematical Experience*. Houghton Mifflin, 1982.

Duckworth, Eleanor. *The Having of Wonderful Ideas and Other Essays on Teaching and Learning*. Teachers College Press, 1987.

Ekeland, Ivar. *Mathematics and the Unexpected.* University of Chicago Press, 1988.

Elementary Science Study. *ESS Tangram Cards, Set I, Set II, and Set III.* Dale Seymour, 1988.

Elmore, Richard, and Milbrey W. McLaughlin. *Steady Work: Policy, Practice, and the Reform of American Education.* Rand Corporation, 1988.

EQUALS Staff. *Assessment Alternatives in Mathematics.* EQUALS/Lawrence Hall of Science, University of California, 1989.

Gardner, Howard. *Frames of Mind.* Basic Books, 1983.

——. *The Unschooled Mind.* Basic Books, 1983.

Giroux, Henry. *Teachers as Intellectuals: Toward a Critical Pedagogy of Learning.* Bergin & Garvey, 1988.

Goodlad, John. *Teachers for Our Nation's Schools.* Jossey-Bass, 1990.

——, Roger Soder, and Kenneth Sirotnik, eds. *The Moral Dimensions of Teaching.* Jossey-Bass, 1990.

Gould, Stephen J. *An Urchin in the Storm.* Norton, 1987.

Greene, Maxine. *Landscapes of Learning.* Teachers College Press, 1978.

Hawkins, David. *The Informed Vision.* Agathon Books, 1974.

Hilts, Philip. *Scientific Temperaments: Three Lives in Contemporary Science.* Simon & Schuster, 1982.

Hirsch, E. D., Jr., ed. *What Your First Grader Needs to Know.* Doubleday, 1991.

——, ed. *What Your Second Grader Needs to Know.* Doubleday, 1991.

Hofstadter, Douglas. *Metamagical Themes: Questions for the Essence of Mind and Pattern.* Basic Books, 1985.

Holt, John. *How Children Fail.* Dell, 1964.

——. *Learning All the Time.* Addison-Wesley, 1989.

Jackson, Philip. *The Practice of Teaching.* Teachers College Press, 1986.

Johnson, George. *In the Palaces of Memory: How We Build the World Inside Our Heads.* Knopf, 1991.

Kagan, Sharon. *The Care and Education of America's Young Children: Obstacles and Opportunities, Ninetieth Yearbook,* Part 1. National Society for the Study of Education/University of Chicago, 1991.

Kamii, Constance, with Georgia DeClark. *Young Children Reinvent Arithmetic.* Teachers College Press, 1985.

Kamii, Constance, with Linda L. Joseph. *Young Children Continue to Reinvent Arithmetic—2nd Grade.* Teachers College Press, 1989.

Kasner, Edward, and James R. Newman. *Mathematics and the Imagination.* Tempus Books of Microsoft Press, 1989.

Kaye, Peggy. *Games for Learning.* Farrar, Straus & Giroux, 1991.

Light, Paul, Sue Sheldon, and Martin Woodhead, eds. *Learning to Think.* Routledge & Kegan Paul, 1991.

Linquist, Mary M., and Albert Shule. *Learning and Teaching Geometry, K–12, 1987 Yearbook.* NCTM, 1991.

Matthews, Jay. *Escalante: The Best Teacher in America.* Henry Holt, 1988.

Medawar, P. B. *Advice to a Young Scientist.* Harper & Row, 1979.

——. *The Limits of Science.* Harper & Row, 1984.

————. *The Threat and the Glory: Reflections on Science and Scientists.* Harper-Collins, 1990.

Moyers, Bill. *A World of Ideas.* Doubleday, 1989.

————. *A World of Ideas,* Vol. II. Doubleday, 1990.

National Council of Teachers of Mathematics. *Curriculum and Evaluation Standards for School Mathematics.* NCTM, 1989.

National Research Council. *Everybody Counts.* National Academy Press, 1989.

National Sciences Education Board/National Research Council. *Counting on You.* National Academy Press, 1991.

————. *Reshaping School Mathematics.* National Academy Press, 1990.

Newman, James R., ed. *The World of Mathematics.* 4 Vols. Tempus Books of Microsoft Press, 1988.

Ohanian, Susan. "Teacher's Notebook." *Learning* 85, November/December, 1985.

Overbye, Dennis. *Lonely Hearts of the Cosmos: The Scientific Quest for the Secret of the Universe.* Simon & Schuster, 1988.

Pagels, Heinz. *The Dreams of Reason: The Computer and the Rise of the Sciences of Complexity.* Simon & Schuster, 1988.

Patterson, Leslie, John Stansell, and Sharon Lee. *Teacher Research: From Promise to Power.* Richard C. Owen, 1990.

Paulos, John A. *Innumeracy.* Hill & Wang, 1988.

Penrose, Roger. *The Emperor's New Mind.* Oxford University Press, 1989.

Peterson, Ivars. *Islands of Truth: A Mathematical Mystery Cruise.* Freeman, 1990.

————. *The Mathematical Tourist.* Freeman, 1988.

Quine, W. V. *Theories and Things.* Belknap Press, 1981.

Reimer, Luetta, and Wilbert Reimer. *Mathematicians Are People, Too: Stories from the Lives of Great Mathematicians.* Dale Seymour, 1990.

Resnick, Lauren. *Education and Learning to Think.* National Academy Press, 1987.

Rothman, Tony. *Science à la Mode: Physical Fashions and Fictions.* Princeton University Press, 1989.

Saunders, Hal. *When Are We Ever Gonna Have to Use This?,* third edition. Dale Seymour, 1988.

Schon, Donald. *The Reflective Practitioner.* Basic Books, 1983.

————, ed. *The Reflective Turn.* Teachers College Press, 1991.

Shekerjian, Denise. *Uncommon Genius: How Great Ideas Are Born: Tracing the Creative Impulse with Forty Winners of the MacArthur Award.* Viking, 1990.

Sowder, Judith, ed. *Setting & Research Agenda.* Erlbaum, 1989.

Steen, Lynn A., ed. *On the Shoulders of Giants.* National Academy Press, 1990.

Stenmark, Jean K., Virginia Thompson, and Ruth Cossey. *Family Math.* Lawrence Hall of Science, University of California, 1986.

Stevenson, Harold, et al. *Making the Grade in Mathematics.* NCTM, 1990.

Trafton, Paul, and Albert Shule, eds. *New Directions for Elementary School Mathematics: 1989 Yearbook.* NCTM, 1989.

Watson, Thomas, Jr. *Father, Son & Co.* Bantam, 1990.

Weber, Roger. *More Random Walks in Science.* Institute of Physics Techno House, 1982.

Wexler-Sherman, Carey, Howard Gardner, and David H. Feldman. "A Pluralistic

View of Early Assessment: The Project Spectrum Approach." *Theory into Practice* 27, Winter 1988.

Wiggins, Grant. "The Futility of Trying to Teach Everything of Importance." *Educational Leadership*, November 1989.

Willoughby, Stephen. *Mathematics Education for a Changing World*. Association for Supervision and Curriculum Development, 1990.

Wilson, James Q. *Bureaucracy: What Government Agencies Do and Why They Do It*. Basic Books, 1989.

Index